the invincibility training: total transformation in 3 days

BAREFOOT DOCTOR

HARPER
element

For Nicola

HarperElement
An Imprint of HarperCollins*Publishers*
77–85 Fulham Palace Road,
Hammersmith, London W6 8JB

The website address is: www.thorsonselement.com

and *HarperElement* are trademarks of
HarperCollins*Publishers* Ltd

First published by HarperElement 2005

10 9 8 7 6 5 4 3 2 1

© Barefoot Doctor, Stephen Russell 2005

Stephen Russell asserts the moral right to be
identified as the author of this work

A catalogue record of this book is
available from the British Library

ISBN-13   978-0-00-720072-6
ISBN-10   0-00-720072-2

Printed and bound in Great Britain by
Martins the Printers Ltd, Berwick upon Tweed

contents

the instructions 193
as a stand-alone section

prerequisite preamble

> Invincibility means the inability to be overcome or the
> ability never to be overcome – by anything or anyone –
> at the deepest level of your being. Whatever happens or
> doesn't happen in your life, you remain in a constant state
> of enlightenment.

author's preface

Myself, I've spent 40 years training in and practising Taoist martial arts and 30 years training and practising various healing arts in the Taoist tradition, supplemented by a fearsome brand of hands-on training in psychotherapy as well as Native American shamanism (having lived for some years in New Mexico). I consider myself a student in these arts who has everything to learn and always will.

An intrinsic aspect of being a student of these disciplines includes passing on what you've learned as freely and generously as possible to as many people as are interested, as clearly and directly as you possibly can. If you don't, your arts dry up and become lifeless.

So being devoted to developing in my practice, I've dedicated my life to sharing as much as I can in as clear and concise a way as practicable through every medium at my disposal to as many people in as many places as possible. I'm always looking for new and improved ways to do this with more and more directness and impact – no matter the medium being used. It has always interested me to see how much I can bend whichever medium I'm using to make the transmission more pure and have more impact.

The Invincibility Training is without doubt the most pure and potentially impactful transmission I've yet managed – in book form at least. It developed from trainings I have done with my closest students over the years and was adapted with the greatest of care and thought to be used at home by pretty much anyone who can read, regardless of their previous experience (or lack of it) in martial arts, healing or any other aspect of Taoist or other spiritual practices.

As stepping into your intimate space for an entire 64-hour time span, is naturally bound to be fraught, with so many variables to consider, it's almost impossible to make the style of instruction to suit everybody. I've done my best and, in my humble opinion, I've done a top job, but inevitably there will be moments of hilarity when you come up against some of the more absurd instructions. It can't be helped.

It turned out to be the most enjoyable book to write of the 10 so far – in fact I can't imagine enjoying writing a book as much, though, of course, I remain open to all possibilities. Hence, I'm expecting it to be at least half as enjoyable to read, which, from my point of view, will be more than enough (again in my humble opinion) to delight and amaze you into declaring, 'Barefoot is a brick!' for all the world to hear.

I imagine it will take a while for people actually to do the training and for the word to spread, but when it does it will be a terrifically exciting movement to watch, because the training is nothing short of a full-blown game of spiritual Twister. Even if you simply read *The Invincibility Training* as a book without doing the training itself, I have every confidence you'll find it a damn enjoyable read. Were it not so, it wouldn't be worthy of being called a book in the first place. Number one rule is it has to be enjoyable to read. And you'll find it immensely useful to boot, in terms of picking up an incredible amount of handy tips for self-development and self-mastery.

But my hope and prayer is that you enjoy reading it so much, you simply can't resist doing the actual training at some point and by so doing get to experience some of the same exhilaration and benefits from being invincible that I am humbly blessed to enjoy myself. And eventually we may all be walking in the realm of the gods but with our feet firmly on the ground. And may this lead to, or be contributory to, the evolutionary process of all humanity.

thankyous

To King Philip, friend and brother on the path, who chummed me along so generously and selflessly through the intensive record 8-solid-day process of writing this book, bought me dinner, satsumas and chocolate, took me driving to clear my head, listened to my fears and doubts, encouraged me when I was flagging and generally bolstered my spirits as only a brother can but even better.

To Carole Tonkinson, my truly wonderful commissioning editor, whose unfailing belief in me made this book a reality in the first place.

To my intrepid PA, Naked Nurse for her consistently unflagging, near-superhuman support in all aspects of my work and holding the fort for me while I was out of the loop writing the book.

introducing *the invincibility training*

opening

Picture this: it's from the *Mahabharata*, the greatest Indian epic poem ever written. Arjuna, the perfect warrior, is about to lead his troops into battle in a civil war between brothers for control of the kingdom. Among those lined up against him on the other side, are cousins, friends and even his spiritual master. Realizing this, he suddenly loses the will to fight, dismounts from his chariot and drops to his knees, immobilized with deep primal fear and anguish. Krishna, a divine messianic being, appears to him there and then on the edge of the battlefield and says:

> 'I am all that you say, all that you think. Everything rests on me like pearls on a thread. I am the earth's scent and the fire's heat. I am appearance and disappearance. I am the trickster's hoax. I am the radiance of all that shines. All beings fall in the night and are brought back to daylight. I have already defeated all these warriors, but he who thinks he can kill and he who thinks he can be killed are both mistaken. No weapon can pierce the life that informs you; no fire can burn it; no water can drench it; no wind can make it dry. Have no fear and rise up, because I love you.'

(From the Peter Brook play version, written by Jean-Claude Carrière, translated by Peter Brook).

Then Arjuna, seeing, as if with Krishna's eyes, through the illusion of physical reality to the truth of his own spiritual nature, goes into battle and though it swings both ways with fearsome force, great violence, injury and loss of life to both sides, he emerges the victor.

By dispelling his version of reality, thus seeing existence from a different angle, the warrior-hero in dread and awe faces his greatest battle, the battle of life itself, finds his spirit within and is invincible. That's the essence of the Invincibility Training in a nutshell.

the training

The Invincibility Training evolved out of running small experimental intensive awareness training sessions with my closest students of martial arts. The result translated into a 3-day training you do on your own, with a partner or friends at home, starting on a Friday evening and ending at work on a Monday lunchtime, during which, hour by hour, you take yourself through a set series of processes involving powerfully transformative, ancient Taoist chi kung (internal and external energy-stimulating exercises) and mental reframing exercises culled from original Taoist martial arts mental training methods, yet adapted for the layperson in modern world.

The processes themselves, while simple to perform and not overtly strenuous are nonetheless challenging enough to make a serious impact at the deepest level. The purpose is to enable you to see through the illusory surface of everyday life, discover your original spirit, which is by nature invincible, and establish a rapport with it that will go on for the rest of your life and enable you to maintain and develop your intrinsic invincibility through thick and thin.

The intended effect is a marked increase of energy, strength, self-confidence, clarity, focus and personal power, and a deep sense of being spiritually invincible come what may – in short, total personal transformation in 64 hours.

- The first 24 hours are allocated to undoing all previous notions of who you are and what reality is. In the mythological terms of the West, this would be akin to the Crucifixion.

1

- The second 24 hours are allocated to re-harnessing all facets of self, according to the Taoist-based blueprint for invincible warrior status – the resurrection.

- The final 16 hours are allocated to assimilating, integrating and celebrating the previous 48 hours of input.

Symbolically speaking, the 64 hours correspond to the 64 hexagrams of the I Ching, the ancient Taoist-Confucianist 'book of changes', an oracle of utmost profundity.

Numerologically speaking, 6+4=10 – take the two digits comprising that: 1+0 = 1 – the starting point of a new level of existence.

Practically speaking, the 64-hour span is the optimum timeframe in which to effectively conduct the training.

Because silence is so rare and yet crucial to accessing the levels of self required to be invincible, Friday evening is spent in total silence, sometimes blindfolded and with earplugs, and is devoted to orienting yourself to the idea of finding a new way of perceiving reality in preparation for the physical and psychological effects of entering a significantly altered state for the next two days.

Saturday until 8 pm is also spent in total silence, during which you gently but effectively deconstruct your previous version of reality until you are fully in neutral in relation to yourself and the world around you, as well as in a state of super-sensory awareness.

Saturday from 8 pm till Sunday at 8 pm is spent creating yourself anew from the core outwards according to traditional Taoist warrior principles, with your original invincible spirit fully in command instead of your self-limiting, finite, localized ego with its petty concerns, fears, doubts, anxieties and neuroses.

Monday till noon, hour by hour, you follow particular processes on your way to work and at work, designed to integrate your newfound perception and stance into the day to day.

---

equipment required

1 blindfold

1 pair of earplugs

1 blanket

1 book of any description, 8-cm thick

1 chair

approximately 4 sq m of clear floor space

1 A4 pad

1 pen

1 music stand per participant (optional)

1 decent sized mirror

3 or more alarm clocks, depending on the number of participants involved.

---

taoism, taoists and the tao – where this all comes from

Around 600 BC and a bit, somewhere in Hunan, China, a guy called Lao Tsu (crudely translated as 'eternal child master') is accredited with compiling or possibly writing the collection of 81 cryptic poems of profound yet simple universal wisdom which comprise the *Tao Te Ching* (again crudely translated as 'book of the way of true virtue' or 'book of the virtuous way'). To date, the *Tao Te Ching* is the best-selling book in the world, even outstripping sales of the Bible. This makes sense when you consider the size of the Chinese speaking population. Not because of this but because he just happened to be in the right place at the right time, Lao Tsu is reckoned as being the godfather of Taoism, although no doubt there were centuries or more of august and accomplished Taoists before him.

Taoism is not a religion in any sense of the word. It is merely a simple blueprint-style philosophy and a collection of techniques for making that philosophy work as a practical tool in everyday life.

Anyone can be a Taoist. You don't have to be Chinese or ancient. You don't have to wear Chinese kung fu costumes or any other form of fancy dress. You don't have to change your diet or take on a set of rules to live by. You can be a practising member of any faith, creed or religion and still integrate Taoist practice fully into your daily repertoire without infringing on the rules or ethics of whichever faith, creed or religion you are a member. No wars have ever or will ever be fought in the name of Taoism. You don't have to join any clubs or toe any line. You don't need to go anywhere particular or be around other Taoists.

The idea behind Taoism is that there is this thing called the Tao (pronounced with a very soft 'T' as in 'dow'). The Tao is a name for something that can't actually be named, or if named can't be described or explained, at least not in terms the mind could understand. It represents that ineffable primordial, pre-atomic force that preceded existence and non-existence and which continues to generate what we experience as reality, in all its myriad aspects, including the phenomena of you and I. Not only does it generate reality, it also informs reality with energy or 'chi', the active agent that causes everything to come into and remain in manifestation. When the chi leaves you, you die. When the chi leaves a planet, it stops spinning. Chi expresses itself through two complementary and opposing forces: yin and yang. Yin represents everything that is feminine, passive, dark and withdrawing – the negative, but not necessarily in a bad sense. Yang represents everything that is masculine, active, bright and outgoing – the positive but not necessarily in a good sense. Incidentally, though I use the words feminine and masculine, this does not correspond to women and men, for women have a balance of both yin and yang running through them and informing them, as do men.

These two forces express themselves visibly in the external world, the 'world of the ten thousand things' or, as I prefer to call it, the world of the world. In the world of the world, everything is relative, hence ultimately illusory. Only the Tao is real and unchanging. The idea of Taoism is to identify with the unchanging Tao instead of identifying with the changing forms of the world of the world, yet still be able to act and conduct yourself with utmost effectiveness in all your engagements with the world of the world.

The Tao operates within every situation that can possibly happen. If you learn to discern its flow in your affairs and, instead of forging your way through life with your will and rational mind alone, divest yourself of vanity and follow its flow, the conditions of your life will be such that you find yourself carried on a current so powerful you can't resist. This eventually leads you to the sea of total enlightenment. At this point you will reach the stage of being a 'Golden Immortal' and are free to roam the celestial spheres on the back of a dragon for eternity.

5

The Taoists developed many methods to achieve this. These include martial arts – Tai Chi, Hsing I, Pa Kua and White Crane, for example; meditation systems – Chi Kung, Red Dragon Yoga, Nei Kung, for example; various healing therapies – acupuncture, massage, herbs, for example; and healing for places – Feng Shui. Along with the Confucians, with whom they have always been intimately connected, as they have with the Buddhists likewise, they passed down an oracle consisting of 64 hexagrams, called the *I Ching*, or Book of Changes, which contains profound wisdom to guide you through the pitfalls of the world. It is upon these 64 hexagrams that the 64 hours of this training are based. Though this will form the basis of another book, should there prove to be a demand for it, this present book is not the place to go into such an in-depth study, so for the moment you'll just have to take my word for it that there is a sound basis to the whole affair.

The point is, Taoist practice, upon which *The Invincibility Training*, is firmly based, is purely an existential experiment. You do the techniques and see what it does before deciding whether it works for you or not. It's as simple as that.

the contract

This training will deliver transformative results, but only if you do the training as instructed. Implicit here is a contract, not only between you and me, though at first glance it might appear otherwise, but also and more importantly between you and yourself. My contract with you is already fulfilled. My part is to provide the necessary content, which I've duly done. Your part is to do whatever you like with it. It's up to you from hereon.

However, I do advise you not to rush blindly into entering the contract on your side before you've had a chance to familiarize yourself with the information, particularly the actual instructions for each of the processes comprising the training and get a sense of how it will feel taking on the commitment of spending what amounts to an unbroken span of 64 solid hours of your life, including sleep and other daily essential activities, retraining your entire being.

If you make up your mind to go ahead, take a piece of paper and pen and write down the following:

'I, [your name here], do hereby solemnly swear to take myself through this training from start to end in one go, following the instructions precisely to the letter. I accept there will be difficult moments and passages and yet am willing to persevere regardless.'

Then sign, date and stow it.

obligatory warning and disclaimer

Some of the processes constituting this training can be physically and psychologically challenging. If, having familiarized yourself with the information enough to get a feel of what will be required, you think you have any physical or psychological condition – or suspect you may have one – that might be exacerbated by doing the training, consult a medical doctor or psychiatrist, as appropriate before attempting it.

Under English law and by the jurisdiction of the English courts, neither Barefoot Doctor (me), nor any company or individual involved in the production, distribution or sale of this book will be held responsible for any injuries to body or mind sustained through failing to consult professional medical advice before starting, or through faulty practice from failing to follow the instructions precisely.

general scheme of presentation of information

The training instructions, printed in one font, are supplemented with a commentary, printed in a separate font to provide with the full background, rationale and intended effects of each process where necessary.

getting the best out of the book
(as principal organ of invincibility training)

Read it (obviously) lightly, cover to cover, skimming freely, alighting on passages, particularly on commentary that grabs your attention, flitting off to others as your fancy takes you, until you've got an initial feel for it as an entity, in the way of making friends. Indeed, great value can be gained from this as with any ordinary personal development manual, whether you eventually decide to go for the training or not. After that it's probably best to leave it alone for a while. Then, when you're ready, read it again, this time paying attention to the actual content in sequence, both the instructions and the commentary, so you know exactly what you're letting yourself in for when you come to do the training – and why. At this point, you're ready to fix the date and enter into the contract with yourself.

Once the date has arrived and all necessary preparations have been made (these will be outlined and explained soon), this book becomes more than something you just read: it becomes the principal organ through which the training is delivered. This means you will be developing a more complex physical and psychological relationship with it than you would with a novel of similar word count, size or bulk. That's because while with a novel you are free to remain relatively static posture-wise, requiring little extra thought about the spatial mechanics of feeding data into your visual cortex, with this book, as principal training organ, you'll be required to carry it with you and have it close to you for 64 hours as you move around making actions and placing yourself in postures not necessarily conducive to the act of reading. This means you'll have to get used to handling and placing the book accordingly as you progress. But it's not rocket science and we both know you'll soon slip into a workable pattern if the will is there. Having said that, it's crucial that you read the instructions carefully and slowly during the training – more than once if necessary. **9**

The commentary is here to inform the training with underlying substance and is not to be read while doing the actual training. The training consists in following the instructions only. For this reason, the instructions have been presented a second time towards the end of the book, without any commentary, in order to help you enter more fully into a meditative state. It will be helpful (but not essential) to have read the commentary assiduously before starting the training. It depends on your style. You might prefer to leave any in-depth journeying till after the event in order to check your own experience against the commentary. Or you may want to do both. Personally, I'd recommend both – but neither is obligatory in terms of the contract.

surrendering to the training

Stripped of any possible hyperbole, this is an intensive training in mind-fulness, lasting 64 hours, equivalent to spending, say, 6 months in a Taoist or Zen monastery. When your thoughts are simple and you are focused exclusively on what is actually going on – as opposed to what you'd like to be going on or wouldn't like to be going on – your vision clears and you see your way through any obstacle. The monkey-like nature of your mind is the only obstacle to this. By surrendering totally to the training for 64 hours, you emerge at the other end transformed in your relationship with ontological reality and with yourself.

At times they may seem absurdly obvious, intricate, repetitive, complex, petty, po-faced or downright bizarre and the timings often apparently arbitrarily quirky. However, the necessary use of detailed instruction to cover every aspect of your existence over a 64-hour time span, is not intended to insult your intelligence, confuse you, brainwash or even amuse you. It is an intrinsic training device employed to get you to tame the monkey mind once and for all.

The Invincibility Training is not something you can half do. You either do it 100 per cent or you don't do it. If, having read and understood this book and agreed with the rationale behind the processes to which the instructions apply, you are then fully willing to surrender the control of the monkey mind to the training for 64 hours instead, you have to follow the timetable and instructions precisely from beginning to end, otherwise there's no point starting it in the first place. A major key to being invincible is realizing that, when seen from the enlightened perspective of the spirit, no single phenomenon is any more important than another. To the trained eye, the Tao, that great unseen generative force, is found and seen as much in the lowliest toilet bowl as in the loftiest mountaintop temple. This is necessarily reflected in the

11

timetable and instructions of the training, so whether emptying your bowels or standing in some ancient Taoist martial stance, all your actions assume equal importance.

It's tempting to tell you to treat it as a game. But it's not a game. It's a life-changing training you either do or you don't. It's as simple as that.

creating the time and space

The training is 64-hours long from door to door and is designed to take place over one weekend, beginning at 8 pm local time on a Friday evening and going through till noon on Monday, the Monday morning module intended for taking to the workplace or equivalent – but this can be adapted to fit around any free 64-hour time span, regardless of which day of the week that might begin, providing you start the training at 8 pm on the first day and finish it at 12 noon on the last day.

In other words, it's not something you just mess about with, so some serious thought should be invested in picking a suitable date within, say, three months of reading the book – but that's entirely up to you. Having gained agreement on it from anyone else you might be doing the training with, and you've decided on a suitable date, book it in your diary or diaries and stick to it.

You will need clear floor space, carpeted or otherwise, of approximately 4 sq m per participant, with enough head-clearance to be able to freely raise your arms above you in standing poses. The space must be well-lit enough to be able to read and see what you're doing, while keeping the lighting as soft, indirect and easy on the eye as possible. The space must be clean and relatively dust and odour-free, ventilated enough to provide an adequate flow of fresh air to breathe deeply while moving freely (and occasionally vigorously), yet warm enough to allow layers of clothing to be kept to a minimum, making sure no energy is wasted maintaining body temperature.

You will also need free and easy access to a functioning bathroom and kitchen, adequate bedding and somewhere to sleep for all participants, bearing in mind that all participants will be required, as part of the training, to bathe or shower and fulfil all other necessary functions, ideally in different bathrooms simultaneously but otherwise, as close together as possible so as not to hold up the process.

preparations

Read the book at least twice.

Procure all your food, drink and any other ingestible matter you and any co-participants require to keep going, along with any other generally necessary provisions including a box of tissues, so there'll be absolutely no need to leave the designated space other than when required as part of a process in the training.

Take care of any outside duties or responsibilities that might otherwise impinge on your unfettered freedom to follow the entire 64-hour training from start to finish. Give due warning to all outside parties who may be concerned you haven't been in touch or returned their calls, that you'll be entirely out of the loop and off the map for the duration of the training. Clear your work and social decks so there's nothing hanging over your head that can't wait till Monday (or the final day of the training) afternoon. Whether doing the training alone or accompanied, arrange for one understanding and reliable friend or family member to be on telephone standby in the unlikely event of anyone participating inadvertently flipping their lid or damaging their body through faulty or improper practice during any of the processes.

- Procure 1 A4 pad and 1 reliable and comfortable-to-use pen per participant.

- Procure 1 mirror per participant, no bigger than approximately 50 sq cm and no smaller than approximately 10 sq cm.

- Procure 2 comfortable, clean blindfolds per participants and 3 sets of foam earplugs or equivalent amount of cotton wool, as individually preferred.

- Procure 1 copy of *The Invincibility Training* for each participant.

- Procure 1 sturdy, full-size, wool blanket per participant.

- Procure 1 average-size book of any description – the contents are immaterial – approximately 8 cm thick, per participant.

- Procure 1 simple kitchen table-style armless chair per participant.

- Procure 1 easy to read from a distance, easy to reset, reliable, preferably silent, alarm clock for the designated space.

- Procure 1 similar alarm clock in the kitchen.

- Procure 1 similar alarm clock for each bathroom likely to be used by participants over the course of the training.

- Procure another similar alarm clock for each sleeping space likely to be used by participants over the course of the training.

- Procure 1 music stand per participant (optional but helpful for reading this book when required to stand hands-free).

- Prepare 2 outfits of comfortable, loose-fitting clean indoor lounging clothes, preferably one dull-coloured to represent letting go of the past, the other bright to represent taking on the new, per participant.

- Prepare 1 regular non-descript street outfit including footwear per participant.

- Prepare 1 relatively discreet social occasion (not too smart, not too scruffy) outfit including footwear per participant.

- Prepare 1 set of work clothes or equivalent, including footwear for Monday (or the final day) if required per participant.

- At some point prior to the first day of training, clear the space of unnecessary clutter and dust, clean, wipe and vacuum all appropriate surfaces and generally air and spruce the place up.

- During the day on Friday (or day on which you're starting the training), eat lunch late enough to be able to hold out for a few hours.

- Avoid any more than a modicum of alcohol or drug intake.

- Avoid any highly starched or greasy food.

- Avoid drinking any more than 2 cups of coffee or 4 cups of tea.

- Prepare a light, easy to digest meal sufficient for all participants to be eaten for dinner on the first night, which can be served up at 10 minutes notice.

- Prepare all necessary crockery, cutlery and glass-wear for the meal.

- Prepare a tray on which to place and carry the meal.

- If doing the training with others, arrange to meet at the designated space at least half an hour before the training starts, so everyone has time to settle in and for which adequate provision has to have been made, so that as far as humanly possible, no one arrives after the training has started.

- Give the space the once over, clearing away any last minute waste or dirt.

- Ensure all requisite equipment is placed in the designated space.

- Place an alarm clock in each bathroom likely to be used over the course of the training.

- Place an alarm clock in each sleeping space likely to be used by participants over the course of the training.

- Place the chair, blanket, 10-cm thick book, pad, pen and tissues in the designated space.

- Put on the duller of the indoor lounging outfits. Keep feet bare.

- Turn off all phones, fixed line and mobile, including for the receiving of text messages.

- Turn off all computers or handheld electronic devices. Turn off all radios including radio alarm clocks that might otherwise go off unexpectedly. Turn off all TV sets.

food and liquids

While specific diet is outside the remit of this training, it is recommended that you keep your intake as light on the liver (not greasy, stodgy or rich), nutritious, fresh, organic, balanced and full of energy as possible. Juicing of fruits and vegetables is advised, as is ingestion of sprouts, pulses and grains. While eating energy-rich foods will certainly enhance your well-being during the training, under no circumstances put yourself under any pressure to alter your diet radically, especially if doing so might endanger your health, (unless, of course, it comprises a preponderance of greasy, stodgy or rich food), as that's not the focus of this training.

Likewise, drink water or fresh juices, jasmine tea, green tea or plain boiled water. Avoid black tea, coffee, alcohol and herbal teas (unless specifically required for health reasons) as much as possible, but don't put yourself under severe strain over this. The idea is to enhance your clarity – not to drive you crazy.

drugs

The same goes for this. Avoid mind or mood-altering drugs, unless medically prescribed, as much as possible (for the same reason as above), but again don't cause yourself stress over it. Ideally, though, it is fully recommended that you do the training straight for best results.

doing the training alone or accompanied

This is entirely up to you and circumstances. Essentially, you're doing the training alone whether in company or not, because each participant will be required to follow his or her own copy of *The Invincibility Training*, precluding the need for anyone reading the instructions aloud and thus assume the role of leader. That would be counterproductive as one of the purposes of this training is to train you to follow your own Tao or way. However, you may prefer to share the experience with others, especially a partner or close friend, in which case it would be preferable were they as committed to doing it as you are. In fact they might enhance the experience rather than detract from it.

Indeed, the more the merrier – facilities and logistics permitting – in terms of the potential synergy produced whenever more than one person focuses on the same thing at the same time. On the other hand, while perhaps slightly more sober-toned, doing it alone encourages a more full-on, one-on-one relationship with the training and will certainly be far simpler in terms of logistics. It's swings and roundabouts and entirely up to you. But if you do go ahead and arrange to do the training with one or more other people, each participant should have had a chance to read and familiarize themselves with the contents of this book and to have undertaken subsequently of their own accord to enter fully into the above-mentioned contract and hence be fully willing to go along with the entire 64-hour process without leaving the designated space unless required to do so as part of a process, otherwise it starts getting messy.

timetable scheme

As well as the obvious training time spent in the designated space going through the various sets of hour-by-hour processes involved, the training takes account of your basic bodily functions, including sleep, eating, drinking, going to the toilet, washing, bathing and even sex, although it is recommended that you abstain from all solo or shared sexual experience until the end of Sunday (or the equivalent last full day of training), for the reason that sexual energy is a potent force and its release to whatever extent over the course of the first 48 hours of the training could upset the highly delicate processes involved, as will become apparent when you get into the training.

It is crucial you stick closely to the set timetable for the sequence of processes throughout the entire 64-hour time span, however exacting, in order for the training to have full impact. Accessing the willingness to stick to the highly precise and exacting timetable is in itself an intrinsic component of the training, as will quickly become apparent and, if adhered to, fundamentally alter your relationship with linear time, giving you full command over it by the end of the training.

in case of forced abortion of the training

If, during the first 48 hours, you are forced to abort the training as a result of emergency or unforeseen contingency, put it down to practice and fix a new date on which to start again. If, however, you are forced to abort during the final 16 hours, it's OK (though obviously not preferable to an all-in-one-go job) to finish the training at a later date providing you refresh the information in your mind by reading the book again to help you return to the appropriate internal state.

handling unexpected external interruptions

Because you don't want to be disturbed at any time in the designated space, particularly between 8 pm on Friday (or the starting point of the training) and 8 pm Saturday (or the first full day of the training), during which you'll be required to remain more or less in total silence, mostly with earplugs inserted and therefore only able to communicate effectively with pen and paper, even when dealing with someone coming unexpectedly to your door. However, it is impossible to preclude the possibility of having to answer the door to the house or to say you should ignore unexpected visitors till they go away – specifically because with your phones and communication devices turned off, it is possible someone is trying to contact you in event of an emergency or unforeseen contingency. For this reason, it would be prudent, during your preparations, to grant a simple rhythmic code to be used when ringing the bell or knocking, to anyone likely to need to use it in event of such an emergency or contingency. Beyond that, it's down to using your intuition.

relaxing throughout

One of the striking differences between Taoist martial arts training, from which *The Invincibility Training* has been culled, and most other martial arts training, is the mutually respectful, mature and well-mannered atmosphere between teacher and student. It is naturally expected that students will discipline themselves if they sincerely wish to lay claim to the skills being taught. It is assumed the student needs no commands shouted by others but that internal commands will be self-issued softly yet firmly, according to the principles of the training.

The very essence and style of Taoist martial art forms, emphasizing, as they do, the virtues of sensitivity, softness, slowness (as in less haste, more speed), humbleness (as opposed to bravado in the face of the Tao), reliance on internal energy (as opposed to external strength to generate personal power), grace (as opposed to force and intelligence rather than brawn), lend themselves perfectly to the development of tenacious strength – the cornerstone of invincibility.

The Invincibility Training involves movements and static postures, at first glance they appear perfectly effortless but because they are re-peated in great number or held for great lengths of time, in practice they are potentially extremely challenging for even the fittest participant. The same holds true for the mental processes involved in the training, which sometimes rely on the ability to repeat certain ideas a relatively enormous number of times or to hold one thought for a relatively enor-mous length of time.

The key to success in this, as with all things, the initial will to succeed notwithstanding, lies in your willingness to relax in the midst of the act. And the key to that, lies in your willingness to let your breath flow freely in and out without hindrance caused by inadvertently tensing your diaphragm and holding your breath, unless specifically required to do so as part of a process. If at any time during the training you feel your breath blocking and your mind and body tensing (or vice versa), relax immediately and allow your breathing pattern to settle down before continuing.

the invincibility training

1

friday (or first day of training)

deconstruction: the undoing process begins

8.00 pm

(The next 24 hours are conducted in total silence. If you've been talking, stop now.)

The purpose of the next 24 hours is to induce your monkey mind to stop chattering long enough for your deeper original consciousness to emerge, whence springs true wisdom, vision and personal power. Observing silence is also likely to cause a notable increase in telepathic ability.

Take stock of where you are and how you feel.

Taking stock is something your mind is attempting pretty much all the time but rarely do you give it the opportunity to feed back its findings to you. Actively taking stock provides this opportunity. However, taking stock does not imply drawing conclusions. Conclusions are impossible while a work is still in progress.

Insert earplugs.

This helps reduce the pull on your vital kidney energy, normally responsible among many other things, for supporting your hearing function. When you relax into muffled sound mode, your kidneys need no longer work so hard in this role and are hence left with more energy for their other responsibilities, such as maintaining the integrity of bones, joints, brain cells, nerves, willpower and reproductive drive.

Stand with feet together in the centre of the designated space facing approximately due north.

Taoist forms traditionally start facing north to avail yourself, face-on, as it were, of the magnetic flow which moves in a southerly direction. Facing north, refuels your chi (energy).

Place palms together in 'prayer position'.

Pressing your palms together, closes a major energy circuit and momentarily unifies body, mind and spirit in humble preparation for a great challenge.

Bow discreetly, acknowledging the four directions, turning slowly to each in turn, starting with north, then east and so on.

Respectfully humbling yourself in the face of the awesome forces of the four directions, causes a momentary awareness of your place in the universe and institutes the correct attitude with which to commence a great challenge.

Turn and face approximately due south, kneel down on the floor, knees together, sit back on your heels, bend at the hips and allow your chest down onto your thighs. (Alternatively, if you find sitting on your heels impossible or unduly uncomfortable, sit firmly into the chair and lean forwards from the hips likewise).

You are facing south to allow the magnetic force to travel up your backbone from north to south. This has a healthily destabilizing effect, just enough to dislodge gently the overall pattern – as if destabilizing an old wall before knocking it down. But it's subtle this stuff and there's no need to bother yourself with such details unless you are somehow strangely fascinated by them.

Rest your hands behind you, on your sacral bone at the base of your spine.

This will act as a weight and help keep your hips anchored to prevent lower back strain.

Feel the stretch across your lower back.

It's actually very rare to experience this opening in the lower back, but the effects can be profound in helping increase circulation of blood and energy in the kidney, sexual and lower intestinal regions.

Visualize your kidneys filling with blood and energy.

Your kidneys provide the base energy that supports all other energies of the body. Your kidneys are generally in a mildly contracted state in unconscious instinctual reaction to being afraid – fear makes your kidneys contract: it's an animal-level reaction. Undo the contraction by doing things like this posture and you undo the seat of the fear itself. Are you ready to release your fear? What would you put in its place? During the course of this training, it is intended you find out.

Count 9 cycles of slow inhalation and exhalation.

The best way to gauge slow is to count 9 seconds on the in-breath and 9 on the out.

Imagine, on inhaling, the breath travelling up the rear of your backbone into your brain to the crown of your head. Imagine, on exhaling, the breath travelling down the front of your backbone to your pelvic floor.

Placing your body in this foetal position helps reinstate the pre-natal energy loop, in which energy travels up the rear of the spine and down the front in a continuous loop whilst in the womb. Its activation through consciously focusing on it returns you to the prenatal state of pure energy, consciousness and love and thus strengthens and defines the 'shape' of your spirit in the face of the great challenge facing you, being alive in a human body in the world of the world.

Raise your chest away from your hips and sit straight.

Keep your buttocks firmly pressed back onto your heels or the seat of the chair as you do this, to help prevent lower back strain or injury.

Using your mind, elongate your spinal column, feeling it lengthen from the sacral bone at the base, through the back of the neck and into the upper brainstem within your skull.

By lengthening your spine, you reduce the compression on your vertebrae, thus enabling energy and nervous impulses to travel more freely in general and specifically along the spinal pathway which is the main energy conduit in the body. Your spine acts like an antenna picking up information from the cosmos through the crown of your head.

29

Using your mind, broaden your pelvic girdle, feeling your hips relax and spread – likewise your shoulder girdle, allowing your shoulders to slump.

Expanding your mainframe in this manner, affords you optimal internal space and thus facilitates optimal energy flow. The more hunched and crumpled you are, the more constricted the flow. Expanding physically instantaneously translates into expanding psychically and energetically.

Feel the energy racing round your brain and chest.

Because you spend so much time thinking, energy is naturally drawn up into your head to support your brain, which is fine as long as you allow it back down again where it belongs in your kidney region so it can be recycled. If you don't let it down, your brain gets overstuffed with it and your thoughts become tangled and knotted. Eventually because your energy is not being efficiently recycled by your kidneys, it dries up and you become physically exhausted.

Allow it to sink downwards and settle around a single point 6 cm below the navel, imagining your pelvic girdle forming a bowl in which to receive it.

This is a crucial key to sanity and internal comfort – allowing the excess energy that gets stuck by default in your brain on account of the habitually chattering monkey mind, to drop into your lower abdominal region, specifically around your *tan tien*, your 'field of heaven', approximately 6 cm below your navel, your body's main energy boosting point, whence it can nurture your kidneys instead, thus helping them perform their vital functions more effectively, specifically in their role of increasing willpower levels in the face of the great challenge.

30

The *tan tien*, or the one point, is the centre from which all movements are made in martial arts and life in general, to cause your entire body and hence, mind, to move as a single unit and thus amass the power of a tidal wave, a crucial aspect of invincibility.

Using your mind, scan all areas of your body for unnecessary muscular tension, starting at the crown of your head and working carefully down to the soles of your feet. Wherever you notice tension, let it go on an out-breath.
Tension constantly accrues in your muscles without your realizing it. This instantaneously translates as tension in your mind. Actively releasing it, specifically in a downward direction like this, is prerequisite before commencing the great challenge, in this case, specifically the training, because if you're not relaxed for it, it will be a drag.

Placing your palms down on the floor either side of your knees to balance yourself, stand up slowly, starting at your hips and slowly straightening your torso to the vertical position, your head coming up last.
Moving slowly and mindfully between positions, between moments, between events, gives rise to continuity of consciousness, without which you tend to fall down the holes between one action and another and often lose yourself for days if not lifetimes.

Keep breathing. While this may seem insultingly obvious, you'd be surprised, if you counted, how many times a day you hold your breath without realizing it. Holding your breath, traps your energy and thoughts and locks them, hence you, into a holding pattern – like a plane that can never quite land. Allowing the breath to flow freely is the key to freedom itself – freedom from self-inflicted suffering caused by the often borderline crazy thoughts and machinations of your monkey mind.

8.07 pm

Why 8.07 and not 8.05 or 8.10? Why be tyrannized by decimals and parts thereof? Time is yours to do what you want with. In any case, 7 minutes is about how long the preceding should have taken. It will seem strange at first to follow time in such minute detail but before many hours have passed, your relationship with time will shift dramatically and you'll feel as if you're dancing freely with it, rather than be under its dominion.

Walk slowly to the bathroom.

No one action is any more important in the great scheme, than any other. Walking to the bathroom, an action you might normally take without much thought, is just as important, being part of your precious life as it is, as any other action – the journey is as important as the destination.

As the weight of your body falls onto your left foot, place awareness in your right hand. As the weight of your body falls onto your right foot, place awareness in your left hand.

This form of body and energy centred contemplation replaces the usual internal chatter of the monkey mind and helps your deeper consciousness connect the disparate parts of you. This one is particularly powerful as it accentuates the natural cross-over energy flow between the two sides of the body and brain.

Your only thought other than that, is, 'I am walking to the bathroom'.

Keeping the internal commentary simple, direct and to the point is an invaluable aid to increasing mindfulness and single focus and helps override the monkey mind's chatter.

Remove clothing. Notice the change of temperature and sensation at the surface of your body. Remove earplugs. Notice the change of sound-level and the effect it has on your senses. Turn on the shower to hot or, if no shower is available, run a hot bath. Empty your bladder and bowels as required.

While it may seem absurd following such potentially intrusive instructions normally associated with personally intimate matters, the effect is to induce a greater degree of mindfulness in every action you take. The Tao is found as much in the toilet bowl as in the temple – perhaps more so – and is worthy of profound respect, as are you, no matter where you are or what you're doing.

Place the book appropriately so as to keep it dry.

It's naturally impossible to guide you specifically as to how to physically deal with the logistics of having the book consistently handy and easily readable as you conduct the processes in the training and some imaginative improvisation on your part will be required, as you're already no doubt discovering. This serves as yet another reminder, were one needed, that there is no such thing as the ideal, other than conceptually.

Check the time on the clock.

Likewise this relationship with the clock's face, which will develop and settle into a workable groove of itself as you go along. Eventually, as the training progresses, you'll not need to look at the clock to know the time precisely. Your unconscious mind is in any case constantly counting the bits, frames and seconds of the movie you're in. Your dialogue with the clock's face you're encouraged to develop here, will trigger your awareness of your own internal clock.

33

8.12 pm

Take a 6-minute shower or bath.
This is a brief yet mindful excursion into aqueous reality only and not intended as a bath-time indulgence. Not everything in the training is done slowly.

Wash your body in a brisk, yet gentle, loving manner, from the head down.
Moving energy from the head towards the toes, calms you. Doing it in the other direction excites your energy. Signalling love and caring to your body rather than impatience or carelessness, soothes your nerves and sends healing messages to that part of your brain dealing with your autonomic functions.

As you wash, say to yourself 6 times, 'I am not only washing the dirt off my body, I am cleansing myself of everything from the past I've been clinging to consciously or unconsciously that no longer fully promotes my well-being.'
You can transform the most apparently mundane, everyday act, such as bathing, into a ritual of deeper significance, simply by declaring it so to yourself in this manner. You define and dictate your reality according to the way you tell yourself it is, during the endless conversations you have with yourself in your head – the chattering of the monkey mind. If you start injecting positive commands into the dialogue, it disrupts the usual line of conversation just like when you say something outrageous or way off-kilter at a dinner party of uptight people. The conversation stalls and in that moment of group embarrassment while everyone's slightly stunned, you can slip in the most profound comments and be heard by one and all. It's a hypnotic technique. All you're doing by making declarations to yourself

is hypnotizing yourself out of one state into a better one. So rather than simply letting your monkey mind wander from tree to tree while you wash your body, you're giving it a different story to tell itself – we're washing off our past here – not just our dirt. This is a spiritual event. Monkey mind likes the sound of that so it shuts up for a minute, engrossed in the difference and then, for that minute at least, comes the peace. Or maybe a minute's stretching it a bit – 15 seconds more like, if you get lucky.

8.18 pm

But however peaceful you are right now, this was only ever going to be a 6-minute bathing session.

Dry off carefully. Apply skin, hair and fragrance products at your discretion. Use all products as if applying healing balms. Apply them lovingly and caringly to yourself. It's a gesture of self-respect. The unconscious urges driving you respond well to such gestures over time.

Replace earplugs. Put your clothes on. Be sensitive to the feel of the clothes against your skin and appreciate it. Appreciating everything means nothing is wasted on you. That's what makes you rich in the world of the world, not money.

8.23 pm

Walk slowly to the kitchen.

Let yourself enjoy the muffled quality of the sound. If you feel panic about it, simply breathe and relax even more. Obviously you can always remove the earplugs at your discretion – they're your ears and your plugs after all – but the help earplugs can give in terms of amplifying inner stillness is worth a bit of aural claustrophobia if you're willing to surrender to it.

As the weight falls on your left foot, place awareness in the right palm. As the weight falls on your right foot, place awareness in the left palm.

Sometimes you'll feel it, sometimes you won't. It doesn't matter. It's all about preparing for spontaneity – in this case the spontaneous criss-crossing of chi from one quadrant of your body to the other, when it happens, through a central fulcrum located at the one point below the navel, producing a magnificent sense of balance.

The only thought in your mind is, 'I am walking to the kitchen'.

When you're walking to the kitchen, you're walking to the kitchen. When you're preparing the meal, you're preparing the meal. Obvious to you now maybe, but how often are you attempting to do 8 things at once and succeeding at enjoying none of them? And if you're not enjoying where you are and what you're doing, even if it's nothing, then what's the point? There isn't one. Enjoyment is paramount.

Get the meal ready.

8.34 pm

Walk slowly to the designated space carrying the meal on a tray. As your weight falls on your left foot, place awareness in the right palm (holding the tray). As your weight falls on your right foot, place awareness in your left palm (holding the tray).

This is extending the walking contemplation into a walking and carrying contemplation.

Your only thought is, 'I am walking to the designated space carrying a meal'.

Of course, you'll have loads of other thoughts along with that but this is the only thought you actively choose to entertain.

Sit comfortably on the chair. Place the tray on your lap. Hold your two hands over the meal, palms facing down, approximately 10 cm above the food.

This is a blessing. There's nothing religious about it. It's merely a gesture of respect to the material reality that supports you, specifically the food it feeds you with. This sanctifies the food. Sanctified food is better for your health. To my knowledge there are no scientific studies to back this up but try it and see for yourself. This is an existential adventure.

Be aware of the work of all the people involved along the chain of getting this food on your plate. Be aware of the intricate forces of nature responsible for its existence. Be aware of how painful it is to be starving.

This isn't to make you feel guilty. Guilt is the last thing I'd want you to invoke right now. Guilt is bad for your digestion of both food and reality in general. This is merely to remind you never to take the food you eat for granted but always appreciate it fully. Otherwise you're missing at least 90 per cent of its life-giving value.

Be aware of the life-giving goodness in the food you are about to be filled with. Be thankful. In your mind, say, 'Thanks'.

The point of saying 'thanks', isn't to appease the gods or the Tao. Neither give a fig for your thanks. They'll keep giving you what you need regardless. But gratitude produces the state of grace and in the state of grace, the air starts sparkling and crackling with chi and wonderful things come into manifestation right before your very eyes.

Feel the subtle force of that gratitude exit through your palms and into the food.

Practically speaking, taking a moment to energize your food before you eat encourages that part of your mind dealing with your autonomic functions to separate nutrients from waste more effectively and assimilate their life-giving properties more efficiently. It also helps you remember how fortunate you are to have something to eat.

Mentally elongate your spine. Broaden your hips and shoulders. Relax your thoracic and abdominal cavities (chest and belly).

Optimizing your physical space, gives your organs and bowels more room in which to do their work; being less cramped – and hence happier – they tend to make a better job of it.

Take a mouthful of food. Be sensitive to the experience of taste and how it immediately affects your state and tone of mind. Relax your jaw.

Without being aware of it, you probably hold excess tension in your jaw, and when in the act of chewing food, this will transmit that tension to your organs and bowels.

Smile with your eyes.

As well as making you feel instantly happier, this causes the muscles of your throat to open and relax, which aids the digestion process. In actual fact, this instruction might better read, 'Smile from deep within your belly and let the smile spread up all the way to the tops of your ears', but it seems too long-winded at this juncture. It's a top tip however. Maybe keep this one for later.

Chew the food in your mouth 18 times.

Traditional Taoists would have you do this 36 times but being a Wayward Taoist and knowing how unusually protracted this would feel these fast-living days, I've halved it for the sake of expedience. Hopefully this will avoid you resisting the idea of increasing chew-factor altogether, though obviously the more times you chew each mouthful – and hence break down the food – the less work your stomach and gastro-intestinal tract has to do, the less strain they experience, hence the more likely you are to avoid triggering stomach and bowel disorders, such as IBS or worse.

Swallow the food.

Mentioned just in case the chewing contemplation held you so entranced you forgot the purpose of it.

Repeat until the meal is finished.

Just couldn't resist that one.

The only thought in your mind is, 'I am eating this food'.

That's right – keep it simple.

Drink some fluid. As you do, the only thought in your mind is, 'I am drinking fluid'. Be thankful for that too. Place both palms on your belly.

Anywhere you place your palms mindfully, will induce the transmission of healing energy. That's why you instinctively put your palm to your head when you bang it – it closes an energy circuit, disrupted by the bang. Placing your palms on your belly, helps your organs and bowels recover more quickly from the bang of the food going in.

Again, be aware of the work of all the people involved along the chain of getting this food on your plate. Be aware of the intricate forces of nature responsible for its existence. Be aware of how painful it is to be starving. Be aware of the life-giving goodness in the food you have just been filled with. Be thankful. In your mind, say, 'Thanks'.

You really can never be too thankful for being here to enjoy the miracle of your own existence. One of the effects of the training is to increase your capacity for gratitude. If you can learn to be grateful for every moment, no matter how much pain you may be in, then nothing can beat you. It's a major key to being invincible.

9.06 pm

Remove both hands slowly.

No rush.

Take hold of the tray. Stand up carefully holding the tray. Walk slowly to the kitchen. As your weight falls through your left foot, place awareness in your right hand. As your weight falls through your right foot, place awareness in your left hand.

You know the routine.

The only thought in your mind is, 'I am walking to the kitchen'. Place the tray down. Walk slowly to the designated space. As your weight falls through your left foot, place awareness in your right hand. As your weight falls through your right foot, place awareness in your left hand. Sit in the chair. Mentally elongate your spine. Broaden your hips and shoulders. Relax your thoracic and abdominal cavities (chest and belly).

This instruction is repeated often, as are many others, because without constant repetition of the most simple principles, you quickly forget – and without the basic structure in place, whatever you build upon it will quickly fall down when the first gust of wind from the world of the world blows through you.

Mentally relax your stomach and intestines.

You probably never think about them much. But think of how much work they do for you, how tirelessly they process your food. Appreciating your organs and bowels makes them feel valued, makes them feel happy – and just like anyone else, when they feel valued, they do a better job. This is basic healing mechanics.

Allow all your mental energy to settle and sink downwards into your stomach and intestines.

This will aid the digestive and eliminative process.

41

Keep breathing.
   You probably already forgot to stop holding your breath.

9.15 pm

Press your buttocks back into the seat of the chair.
   This is to stabilize your sacrum to preclude the possibility of back injury when bending forward.

**Relax your arms and let them hang by your sides. Lean forward from the
hips until your hands are hanging by the sides of your shins just below
knee-level. Make loose fists. Relax your shoulders, elbows and wrists.
Pound a gentle, steady drum roll on the fleshiest part of the ridges of muscle, to the outside of the shins just below knee-level.**
   The energy points you stimulate like this relate to digestion and its
   function of transforming nutrients back into pure energy.

Keep breathing.
   Again, you probably already forgot to stop holding your breath.

9.19 pm

Stop pounding suddenly.

You'll probably feel a strong fizzing sensation in your lower legs as the energy stimulated is released into your system. Make sure you give yourself a moment to enjoy it and follow the way it spreads.

Raise your torso slowly to the upright position. Stand up slowly, your head coming up last.

Leaving your head till last, once the rest of you is fully vertical, places the least amount of strain on your spinal column and upper back muscles.

Walk slowly to the kitchen. As your weight falls through your left foot, place awareness in your right hand. As your weight falls through your right foot, place awareness in your left hand. Take the remains of the meal from the tray. Wash the dishes or rinse and place them in a dishwasher. Relax your body, especially your shoulders and lower back. Keep breathing. The only thought in your mind is, 'I am washing the dishes'.

Washing dishes is cleansing and relaxing for the soul if you let it and ordain it be.

Walk slowly to the bathroom.

Is your monkey mind resisting? Relax, detach, observe and notice the resistance. Make no judgement and don't try to change it.

As your weight falls through your left foot, place awareness in your right hand. As your weight falls through your right foot, place awareness in your left hand. The only thought in your mind is, 'I am walking to the bathroom'. Empty your bladder and bowels as required. Wash your hands. Dry your hands. Rub oil or moisturizer into them.

Treat this as a small gesture of love and respect towards yourself.

Wave hello to yourself in the bathroom mirror.

There's no need to treat yourself like a stranger after all.

Walk slowly to the designated space. As your weight falls through your left foot, place awareness in your right hand. As your weight falls through your right foot, place awareness in your left hand. Your only thought is, 'I am walking to the designated space'.

9.45 pm

Set the alarm clock in your designated space to go off at 10.00 pm. Spread the blanket on the floor. Place the approximately 8-cm thick book on the blanket in place of a pillow. Take a blindfold.

This is merely an aid to induce you to sink deeper within and to divest yourself momentarily of familiar reference points by which you normally define your reality and, by extension, yourself.

Lie down on the blanket, face up, knees bent and soles of the feet flat on the floor.

Lying with your knees bent, rather than with your legs straight out, places far less strain on the back as it flattens out the arch formed by the angle of your sacrum in relation to your lumbar vertebrae.

Read the following instructions, from, 'apply the blindfold', up to 'remove the blindfold', carefully 3 times through, picturing what it looks like and memorize. Apply the blindfold. Place your two palms on your lower abdomen below the navel so the fingertips of both hands meet, little fingertips lightly touching the top of your pubic bone. Adjust your earplugs if necessary. Inhale fully.

This is the only time you make a noise till 8 pm tomorrow. It is inserted at this point to provide contrast and to remind you that you could still make a noise if you really wanted or needed to.

Start humming a continuous 'mmm' sound in a register comfortable for your voice, at moderate volume, until all the air is emptied from your lungs. Become aware of the vibrations this causes in the forehead and cheekbones. Repeat this inhalation and humming cycle twice more.

This will clear your head like a dose of smelling salts.

Let your thoughts drift wherever they want to go (until alarm goes off).   **45**

10.00 pm

Remove the blindfold.

You are playing with your senses here – making sound in the midst of a silent phase will stand out and have more impact on altering your state, especially as this sound causes your skull to vibrate from within – letting in the light after the darkness likewise. It's all to do with the shock of contrasts right now. All part of the undoing process. Go with it.

Stand up slowly, head coming up last. Relax your shoulders, elbows and wrists. Lightly place the tip of the forefinger of each hand at the outer corners of your eyes on each side. Stroke ever so softly and slowly along the edge of the bone immediately under each eye until your fingertips are touching the top of your nose on each side by the inner corner of each eye. Stroke softly and slowly along the edge of the bone immediately above each eye until your fingertips are once again at the outside corner of each eye. Repeat this cycle slowly, softly and patiently 18 times. The only thought in your mind is counting the cycles.

This self-massage technique helps flush away stale blood and energy from the ocular region and encourage the flow of fresh blood and energy instead, thus strengthening the eyes and keeping them youthful. And the direction of the passes, under and over each eye, helps reduce and prevent wrinkling and lines.

Set the alarm to go off at 10.33. Read the following instructions, from 'apply blindfold' up to 'remove the blindfold', carefully 3 times. Picture what it looks like and memorize. Apply blindfold. Stand with feet at shoulder width. Bend your knees. Listen within to the rhythm of your heartbeat.

This requires sensitivity and letting go of irrational fear about your heart stopping.

Start swaying at the hips to the beat of your heart. Allow the movement to grow of itself.

Be sensitive.

Let your arms go. Dance.

Don't worry about what you look like. It doesn't matter. This isn't a dance competition. This is communing with your own heart. It's powerful when you let go.

Express yourself freely. Your only thought is, 'I'm dancing to the beat of my heart'.

This is an instant way of unifying yourself into a single autonomous, rhythmically self-reliant force. I could go on for hours about how, when you dance to the beat of your own heart through daily life, there's nothing that can stop your joy and all that stuff – but really it's best to try it for yourself, see what it does and make up your own mind.

10.33 pm

Stop dancing. Let your breath and energy settle. Remove the blindfold. Walk slowly around the designated space in a counter-clockwise circle.

Walking a circle in a counter-clockwise direction releases negativity and sets you free of the hold of the past.

47

As the weight falls through your left foot, place awareness in your right hand. As the weight falls through your right foot, place awareness in your left hand. Keep breathing. Simultaneously, concentrate your mind on a point, 6 cm below your navel. Walk, moving from this point.

Taking on two or more contemporaneous contemplations is upping the ante in relation to taming your monkey mind. This point, your *tan tien* (the 'one point'), is the point through which heaven, or your inner guiding spirit, commands the movements of your body. By placing some degree of awareness in it at all times, all your movements will be true, graceful, focused and unified – your thoughts, words and deeds likewise.

As you walk in counter-clockwise circles, tell yourself you are progressively stepping out of the past and leaving behind any energetic, psychic, intellectual, emotional, personal, professional and social ties that no longer serve your best interests.

Let yourself enter a mild trance state as you walk. Let your gaze be soft.

Keep one eye on the time.

10.49 pm

Stop where you find yourself. Freeze in the position for a moment. Let your energy settle and your breath normalize. As soon as you feel still within, take the A4 pad and pen. Sit in the chair. Lengthen your spine. Broaden your hips. Broaden your shoulders. Relax your muscles. Keep breathing.

These instructions are repeated with great frequency throughout the training, not to be patronizing or suggest you suffer from amnesia in any major way, but without constant repetition these major basic principles upon which the entire Taoist system rests, are easily overlooked and forgotten.

Keep an eye on the clock. Write a list of everything that comprises your life, including your body, your possessions, your home, your relationships and your education.

This isn't something anyone else is going to see unless you want them to, so indulge yourself and list every single aspect of your life you can think of, by which you tend to identify yourself – your looks, your hair, your body, your clothes, your exercise routine, your diet, your relationships, your home, your possessions, your work, your holidays, your interests, your beliefs, your fears, your likes, your dislikes, your habits, your opinions – all of it.

11.01 pm

Detach the page or pages on which you've written. Hold them in your right hand.

This is partly just moody, partly because your right hand is traditionally the hand you give with and you are about to give this lot up.

With your left hand, place the pad on the floor by your side.

That's just pure moody – the left-hand thing.

Stand up slowly. Hold the list up before you at chest height and tell yourself, 'The value I see and feel in all these aspects of my existence, is the value I have given them'.

This is the start of a structural dislodging process designed to help with the realization that reality as you experience it, reality including you, that is, is merely subjective, mostly predicated on a set of opinions, and that by shifting your viewpoint, you shift the way you experience reality and your place in relation to it, which ability is fundamental to gaining invincibility, in the metaphysical flexibility it affords you. So if the winds of destiny blow you one way, you go with it and land on your feet, if it blows you another, you go that way and land on your feet. But you can only land on your feet if you're flexible and supple enough to bend and blow from one position to another without losing your balance.

Stow the list. Stand facing approximately due north. Place your palms together in 'prayer' position. Bow gently from the waist to the north. Bow to each of the other 3 directions, starting with east.

This is to thank the forces of the four directions for co-operating with you and is committed as an act of self-humbling respect to the Tao. It has all the ritual force you give it. Essentially, though, it serves to connect you in friendship to all parts of the designated space so you don't feel like a stranger – so you feel you've laid claim to it.

Place your awareness in the point 6 cm below your navel. Initiating the movement from this point, turn out all the lights and walk slowly to the bathroom. Until further notice, whatever your eye falls on, tell yourself, 'I have given this all the value it has for me'.

This represents a radical shift of perspective. To take on that you have invested everything you see with the value it has for you, rather than

50

what you see having any actual intrinsic value of its own, means you are in command of your experience of reality in the world of the world. I'm not saying it's right or even true. It's just a way of repositioning yourself for purposes of undoing the rigidity of your mind and mental constructs.

Empty your bladder and bowels as required.
For example, look into the toilet bowl and say within, 'I have given this all the value it has for me'.

Wash and do your essential bathroom routine. Adjust your earplugs if necessary. Silently say goodnight to yourself in the bathroom mirror.
Goodnight.

11.15 pm

If a hot drink or snack is required, walk slowly to the kitchen and prepare it. Remember, until further notice, whatever your eye falls on, tell yourself, 'I have given this all the value it has for me'. When you've done that or if no hot drink or snack was required, initiating the movement from the point 6 cm below your navel, walk slowly to your sleeping place. Again, remember, until further notice, whatever your eye falls on, tell yourself, 'I have given this all the value it has for me'. Remove clothing.
Enjoy being naked for a moment. Don't hide it from yourself.

Put on nightwear if required. Set the alarm for 7.23 am.

These odd times stick in your mind way better than the regular 7.25s, 7.30s and what-have-you. I got the habit from flying around a lot and often marvelling that a flight from, say, Amsterdam to Bangkok, scheduled to arrive at 16.04, actually did land at precisely 16.04 – and reckoned if it's good enough for KLM, it's good enough for me.

Get into bed.

Nice?

Lie back against the pillows, facing up. Keep breathing. Decelerate your breathing.

The slower you breathe, the longer you live – this based on the Taoist idea that you're only granted a limited number of breaths per lifetime, so the quicker you use them all up, the sooner you leave the planet.

Tell yourself, 'I now sleep deeply through the night and remain conscious as I dream and awake 6 full minutes before the alarm rings, feeling re-freshed, rejuvenated, revitalized and ready for anything'.

Affirmative auto-suggestion is particularly effective when repeated just before sleep. The result may not be immediate, however. Often you must repeat an affirmation 3 nights running before it lodges in your unconscious and starts to work. Do not be dismayed if you find yourself buzzing and unable to sleep. If you do get an insomnia at-tack, simply enjoy the altered state of being up in the night and carry on as you were. Treat the time as if you are in a dream, which as well you know, in reality, you are.

Read the following instructions 3 times carefully from, 'place the book down', up to, 'pick up the book and open it,' and memorize. Place the book down. Turn off the light. Close your eyes. Take stock of where you are and how you feel. Sink your consciousness back into the centre of your brain.

This is a crucial key to self-mastery. The more you practise it, the faster it becomes central to your moment-by-moment experience of reality.

As if you had a third eye in the centre of your forehead, gaze out through it at the darkened room.

If you catch this one right, you will actually find yourself looking at the room in all its details through the centre of your forehead. Some details might be subtly different as you are, to all intents and purposes, in the dream state. Often a great light will flood your inner vision, which can easily be mistaken for having forgotten to turn off the bedroom light. If possible, remember not to wake up mistakenly to turn it off. Using this technique will encourage conscious mindful dreaming. Conscious, mindful dreaming is important in training you to be conscious and mindful in the dream of everyday life.

Just before falling fully asleep, turn onto your right side.

This is to encourage the blood into your liver to be purified as you sleep, rather than into your heart, where the excess will give you crazy dreams.

saturday (or second day of training)

deconstruction: the undoing process deepens

7.17 am

Wake up. Take stock of where you are and how you feel.

Probably a bit all over the place to begin with.

Pick the book up and open it. Tell yourself, 'I choose to enjoy this day come what may', 6 times.

Actively choosing the kind of day you want to have, or at least the tone of it, always produces the desired result.

Lightly place the tip of the forefinger of each hand at the outer corners of your eyes on each side. Stroke ever so softly and slowly along the edge of the bone immediately under each eye until your fingertips are touching the top of your nose on each side by the inner corner of each eye. Stroke softly and slowly along the edge of the bone immediately above each eye until your fingertips are once again at the outside corner of each eye. Repeat this cycle slowly, softly and patiently 18 times. The only thought in your mind is counting the cycles.

Waking up is a good time to do the eye-socket massage, as it clears away all stagnant blood from sleeping and wakes your eyes up for the day. One of the most striking symptoms of tiredness, is scratchy, sore eyes. Smooth away soreness with the massage, and you generally no longer feel tired. Or you may but you won't care so much. While these techniques have specific effects, they are included in the training mostly for their value in increasing mindfulness.

Remove earplugs. Place your palms over your ears. Press in to muffle the sound of the room. Remove the palms 1 cm or so to let in the sound of the room. Press in again and so on 18 times.

Your ears are kidney shaped. According to the Taoists, this is no accident as your ears are the external 'flowers' of your kidneys. This exercise is not only good for increasing the protective energy around your ears – thus helping to attenuate the harmful effects of loud noise, as well as reducing the irritation of tinnitus – it also helps boost your vital kidney energy, itself responsible for the general strength and well-being of your entire person. And specifically the health and integrity of your bones, joints, nerves, brain cells and reproductive drive, as well as supplying your willpower and even determining the length of your natural lifespan.

7.30 am

Rolling to one side or the other, slowly get out of bed.

Avoid sitting straight up to get out of bed, or any time you've been lying down on your back, as this can easily strain the small muscles of your lumbar region and shoulder-girdle, which have been lying still and therefore possibly stiff all night.

Take the book. Moving your body from the one point 6 cm below your navel, walk slowly to the bathroom.

The more often you concentrate on bringing awareness to the one point, the more you find yourself naturally moving from it all the time and enjoying the benefits of self-mastery that this confers, but initially you have to think about it a lot.

The only thought in your mind is, 'I'm walking slowly to the bathroom from the one point'.

These simple thoughts are to help keep the internal commentary on reality, so assiduously insisted on by monkey mind, as clear as humanly possible. Clarity of mind is an essential component of invincibility.

Empty your bladder and bowels as required. Wash, shower and take care of all the essentials. Dry off and put on the duller of the two indoor lounging outfits again.

You're still heavily in the letting go process here and the dullness is to signify that.

Put in fresh earplugs. Look around you. Remember, until further notice, whatever your eye falls on, tell yourself, 'I have given this all the value it has for me'.

At first this idea can be unsettling as it implies repositioning yourself in relation to the external world, making the latter seem a lot less solid and reliable. But as you get used to it, you start to feel the possibility of seeing that it's you who commands your version of reality and all the bits and pieces in the world of the world that appear to comprise it, as opposed to the other way round. There are immense advantages to reality and its constituent parts being pliable, especially if you like your existential adventures on the large side.

7.59 am

Moving from the one point 6 cm below your navel, walk slowly to the kitchen. The only thoughts in your mind are, 'I am walking slowly to the kitchen' and 'I have given this all the value it has for me', in respect of whatever your gaze falls upon.

Introducing two almost simultaneous thoughts helps cancel out the machinations of the monkey mind – just one reason it helps walking slowly, so you have time to fit all the thoughts in. Through the training, you gradually introduce more and more simultaneous contemplation motifs until monkey mind has a whole new story to tell itself altogether – and probably a much better, well-rounded one at that.

Make hot and cold beverages as required and drink.

And think, 'Here I am drinking my hot or cold beverage as required'.

8.15 am

Set the alarm in the kitchen for 8.45 am. Do whatever you like till the alarm rings. Do not eat. Do not leave the house. Your only thought is, 'I am now doing whatever I like'.

This is to provide a space in which to observe your reaction to having submitted your will to the training programme and it should provide some insight into the way your monkey mind rebels. Do not ignore Monkey's complaints however. Listen and acknowledge everything Monkey has to say. Just answer each with, 'I am now doing whatever I like'.

57

8.45 am

Walk into the designated space. Stand with feet together facing approximately due north. Place hands together in 'prayer' position. Bow to the north. Turn and bow to the east. Turn and bow to the south. Turn and bow to the west.

This ritual is like placing yourself under the direction of the master, in the traditional martial arts sense – not me, I'm just a student myself – but the master within, or wherever the master should choose to show himself or herself.

In fact, one of the most splendid aspects of practising Taoist martial arts is that they provide a conduit for the spirit of the master to be channelled through. It's not something you have to imagine or make happen. It just happens of itself the more you practise the forms. Your body and mind are taken over for the duration of the practice by the benign presence of a master – someone who through Taoist practices has managed the immortality trick and is thus able to cross the divides of time and space and enter whoever is providing suitable access at the time. This same effect will occur during the training at certain moments. Be on the look-out but don't try and look for it or it probably won't happen – that would equate to Monkey being too noisy.

Whatever your gaze falls upon, tell yourself, 'I have given this all the value it has for me'.

It needs repeating and repeating as a way of continually illuminating your mind from different angles with the same radical idea.

Adjust the lighting and temperature as required. Arrange blanket on the floor. Lie down on your back, knees bent, soles of your feet flat on the floor. Allow your lower back to broaden and sink into the floor. Keep breathing.

In order to gain full value from the process and prevent strain or injury, it's fairly crucial that your focus remains on keeping as much of the surface of your lower back on the floor as possible, throughout the following movement. Indeed, any time you feel back strain, this lying down flat with your knees up, soles flat on the floor and a book under your head, is something you should do for 40 minutes or so and as often as not the pain seems to magically vanish because of the way it aligns your vertebrae.

Place your arms by your sides. Moving from the one point 6 cm below your navel, slowly raise your torso off the floor until you feel the muscles in your belly contract.

This is a simple Taoist sit-up, in case that sounded complicated. **59**

Keep breathing.

Holding your breath during exercise is deleterious to cardiovascular, respiratory and nervous systems.

Relax all muscle groups not being used actively in the raising motion, especially the back of your neck. Hold the posture. Breathe slowly.

This should be enjoyable, not a struggle with yourself. The more you relax and allow yourself to enjoy the sensation of meeting your own body in action, the more effective the exercise will be. The intention is to strengthen the core muscles around the one point, as the stronger this region becomes, the more centred you'll be, hence the more integrated and powerful in all your thoughts and actions.

Count 18 cycles of inhalation and exhalation.

In Taoist numerology, the number 9 is significant for its strength-giving properties. Most strengthening exercises are repeated in multiples of 9 or held for the duration of multiples of 9 breath cycles. The significance of twice times 9, is merely that 18 breath cycles are pretty much the perfect length of time to hold this posture.

Lower your torso slowly till your entire back is lying flat again. Let your lower back sink into the floor. Lengthen your spine. Relax everything. Keep breathing.

Make sure you allow yourself to enjoy the sensation of release. Enjoying it at least trebles the intended healing effect.

Count 3 cycles of inhalation and exhalation.

This gives your body and mind time to integrate the information rush triggered by the movement.

Repeat the entire process of raising, lowering, resting and raising the torso 9 times.

There is no doubt that unless you're relatively fit – and I can't assume you are – this will probably be tough for you. This is why it's so important you take it slowly and remain mindful, as well as remembering to work with your body rather than against it. If you experience untoward twinges of pain, stop and consider seeking medical advice. I have to keep saying that but really you'd have to be pretty cack-handed to injure yourself doing this if you follow all the instructions carefully enough – especially all the emphasis being on gently and slowly.

Place your palms either side of the one point below your navel.

This helps to focus awareness here, which draws energy to it from all around your body, whence it strengthens your core.

Mentally repeat the word 'strength' 9 times.

The unconscious part of your mind which controls your autonomous functions, responds to simple positive ideas, as contained in a single repeated word. Otherwise Monkey will be complaining and wanting to do something less strenuous or exacting and then you're fighting yourself which not only reduces the effect of the process, but also it can be damaging – as all fights usually are.

Turn onto your front.

Look at the world from here right now – the floor and all that. It's important to note everything and acknowledge it. Notice if preferences come up. I prefer being on my back to being on my front, for instance. Simply notice – don't do anything about it – don't judge yourself for it. Relax, detach, observe and notice – that's the way we do it here.

Stretch your legs out straight behind you, feet together. Place your palms on the floor, just to the outside of your shoulders. Lengthen your spine, especially the back of your neck.

In order to gain maximum benefit and avoid strain or injury, it is important you don't default to shortening and compressing your spine while making the following move.

Keep breathing. Pull your buttocks and the muscles of your lower back inwards towards the spine.

You have to visualize and feel this as you're doing it. It's really just a matter of contracting the muscles so you feel them wrap around the core.

Moving from the one point below your navel, slowly raise your torso approximately 10 cm from the floor.

This is a Taoist cobra position.

Maintain the inward pull of the buttocks and lower back muscles. Relax all other muscle groups, especially at the back of the neck. Use the power in your lower back to hold your torso up, rather than relying on your arms. Breathe more slowly.

This must be done by lengthening and expanding into the movement rather than shortening and contracting your way into it.

Count 9 cycles of inhalation and exhalation. Lower your torso slowly to the floor. Repeat the sequence 3 times through.

If, as with any of the processes in this training, you experience undue pain, sickness or dizziness, stop and if necessary contact your GP or medical advisor. But again, it must be said that unless you follow the instructions carelessly it would be hard to cause yourself damage like this, otherwise people would be hurting themselves every time they engaged in face-to-face sexual intercourse, as this is one of the prime moves involved, if you think about it. But don't think about it now.

Focusing awareness on your buttocks and lower back, mentally repeat the word 'strength' 9 times. Roll to your right and lie on your back. Bend your legs at the knees. Place your soles flat on the floor, legs together. Take stock of where you are and how you feel. Allow your lower back to sink into the floor.

Feel your spine realigning itself, gently lengthening progressively from sacrum to skull with every breath you take and release.

Stretch your arms out to the sides, perpendicular to your torso to form a 'T'.

Take a moment to enjoy the sensation of opening across your chest and shoulder-girdle.

Turn your head to face your right hand. Turning from the one point below your navel, let your legs, with knees together, slowly fall over to the left until your left knee is on the floor. Place your left palm on the upper side of your right knee.

This acts as a weight to give more leverage to the stretch.

Keep breathing. Feel the stretch across your torso, especially around the left side of your chest and left armpit. Feel the stretch through your right hip.

Don't fight it. Surrender and release into it. If you experience any untoward twinge in the lower back or shoulder blade region, stop immediately and consider seeking medical advice. But do it gently, slowly and sensitively and it's highly improbable that this will be necessary.

Breathe more slowly. Count 9 cycles of inhalation and exhalation. Moving from the one point below your navel, slowly draw your legs straight and turn your head till you are gazing up at the ceiling. Turn your head to face your left hand. Turning from the one point below your navel, let your legs slowly fall over to the right until your right knee is on the floor. Place your right palm on the upper side of your left knee. Keep breathing. Feel the stretch across your torso, especially around the right side of your chest and right armpit. Feel the stretch through your left hip.

Enjoy both.

Breathe more slowly. Count 9 cycles of inhalation and exhalation. Moving from the one point below your navel, slowly draw your legs straight and turn your head till gazing up at the ceiling.

This move opens your thoracic cavity as well as stretching your lumbar region and is hence beneficial to lungs, heart and, to a lesser extent, kidneys. It also helps energetically to open the door for your love to flow through more freely.

Place both palms on your chest.

Wherever you mindfully place your hands, healing energy will be transmitted.

Mentally repeat the word 'strength' 9 times. Remove palms from chest. Roll to your left.

The significance of rolling is to prevent strain on your lower back when standing. The significance of rolling first to the right and then to the left is merely arbitrary and to keep things balanced and fair between your two sides. Every detail is important in the training.

65

Come onto all fours. Let your head hang down. Relax the back of your neck. Keep breathing.

This is a most effective resting posture. It takes you back to when you were small and used to spend lots of time on your hands and knees and therefore serves to connect you with your more primal, childlike self. Spend a moment enjoying it.

Moving from the one point, slowly stand up. Fold and stow the blanket. Your only thought is, 'I am folding and stowing the blanket'.

9.10 am

Moving from the one point, walk slowly to the bathroom. Remove earplugs.

Enjoy the rush of energy in your head as the sound opens up.

Empty your bladder and bowels as required. Relax.

Remember that you can see the Tao as clearly in a toilet bowel as a temple. No part of your experience of the moment must be denied, otherwise you are casting away parts of your life – and it's the only one you have, so you shouldn't consider wasting any of it through denial. Everything must be acknowledged without prejudice. The Tao is in everything. Were it not so, nothing would exist. Nothing does exist as well, of course, and that's the Tao too, but that's another story for another time.

Keep breathing. Wash. Nod hello to yourself in the bathroom mirror.

I haven't inserted the 'dry off' instruction again since I'm assuming you've picked up and inculcated that bit already by now.

Put in a new pair of earplugs or cotton-wool equivalent.

Note the head sensation caused by closing the sound down again. Are you getting used to it? Are you enjoying it? Don't answer immediately.

9.30 am

Moving from the one point, walk slowly to the kitchen. The only thought in your mind is, 'I am walking slowly to the kitchen'. Set the alarm to go off at 10.20 am. Prepare breakfast. The only thought in your mind is, 'I am preparing breakfast'. Place it on a tray and carry it into the designated space. Sit in the chair and place the tray carefully on your lap.

The reason it's suggested you always eat in the designated space is that it's assumed you may well be using your main living area as the designated space and you may not have a handy clutter-free table at which to eat. If you do, however, from now on feel free to eat at that table. The tray on the lap instruction is merely to arrive at the lowest common denominator eating facilities-wise and is inspired by egalitarian sentiments only. Eating like this won't actually make any difference to any future invincibility levels. What will is how attentive and mindful you can be, wherever you sit to eat.

Place your palms approximately 10 cm above your food. Think of all the energy involved in getting this particular food onto your plate. Think of all the people involved in the chain that made it possible. Think of the forces of nature required for this particular food to exist. Think of how painful it must be to starve. Be thankful for the food you are about to eat. Let the essence of that gratitude stream out through your palms into the food. Eat breakfast. Chew each mouthful 18 times. Tell yourself, 'I have given this taste all the value it has for me.'

Even challenging the very sanctity of the taste of your breakfast here – it's all just a series of opinions you've held, so no need to worry about disloyalty to any particular cereal brand by questioning its intrinsic value. This is all just an existential adventure.

Otherwise, the only thought in your mind is, 'I am eating breakfast'. When you've finished eating, do whatever you like till the alarm goes off. The only thought in your mind is, 'I am doing whatever I like'.

Again, because it's relatively early on in the training, it's important to give Monkey a moment in which to rebel and say hello to itself again. I hope you don't mind or take offence at me calling it Monkey. Personally I think it makes the whole idea of taming it a lot more palpable. And Monkey will also respond much better to training if it knows you love him or her. Firm but loving is the way. The important thing is to witness Monkey doing that and whatever else it does to grab your attention, from the centre of your brain and not get caught up in dialogue with it. You command, Monkey obeys, is the general rule. Otherwise it will revert to how it was before this – Monkey commands, you obey. Which would you rather it be? Because there's nothing in between. Well in reality, there's a lot in between – a bit of Monkey in the driving seat, a bit of you – but here at the level of making a choice that will profoundly influence the way Monkey and you coexist, it's either one way or the other. Choose you, would be my advice but, as always, you must decide for yourself.

10.20 am

Moving from the one point, walk slowly to your designated space. Take the pad and pen. Sit in the chair. Relax. Keep breathing. Lengthen your spine. Broaden your hips and shoulders. Make a list of everything bad or wrong about yourself. Absolutely everything.

> This list is purely subjective. Writing it doesn't set your faults in stone. To the contrary, it helps dissolve the hold you've given them on your mind. Remember, this is only for your eyes so free yourself of inhibitions and let all your self-recrimination pour out now. It's therapeutic.

Don't hold back. Keep breathing. When you finish, sit still. Your only thought is, 'I'm sitting still'.

> There is no judgement at this point. Simply sitting with it and continuing to breathe is enough.

10.40 am

Read each entry on the list. After reading each entry, mentally say, 'I have given this all the negative value it has for me'.

> This thought helps reclaim the power you've given all your perceived faults and shortcomings. At first it may feel unsettling to think, but persevere nonetheless. Don't think about it too much – just say it to yourself and let the words and concept float around your mind of its own accord.

Stow the list. Make a list of everything good or right about yourself. Absolutely everything. Don't hold back.

Don't be afraid to let your head swell a bit. We often have a hard time acknowledging our self-perceived strengths and good points, for fear we may be indulging in conceit. Release yourself from that concept momentarily and indulge in some frank positive self-appraisal.

Keep breathing.

The excitement or nervousness you may feel thinking about your good points may cause you to forget to breathe freely.

When you finish, sit still. Your only thought is, 'I'm sitting still'.

No judgement is required at this point – merely observation.

10.58 am

Read each entry on the list. After reading each entry, mentally say, 'I have given this all the positive value it has for me'.

Why should your self-perceived positive qualities be any less subjective than your negative? Both are merely based on opinions formed more or less spuriously according to the camera angle and lighting at the time. Neither is concrete. Which isn't to say you don't possess those fine qualities. I have every confidence you do. Same for the negative ones. The point is to realize that what you are is neither these qualities nor these faults.

Stow the list. Slowly, moving from the one point, stand up. Slowly walk in a counter-clockwise circle 6 times around the designated space, arms by your sides, palms facing the floor, leaving space for a small apple in each armpit. As you walk, tell yourself you are stepping out of the loop formed by everything you have hitherto considered bad or wrong about yourself, as well as everything good or right.

This is to step out ritually and energetically of the hold the past has on you and free you from the grip of any opinions you hitherto held on to.

11.15 am

Sit in the chair. Push your buttocks back firmly into the seat. Hang your arms by your sides. Make loose fists. Moving from the one point, lean your torso forwards until your fists are hanging by that relatively fleshy muscle mound just below knee-level to the outsides of your shins. Rhythmically pound with your fists on the fleshiest part of the ridge of muscle running down the outside of each shin just below knee-level.

As well as being beneficial to your digestion, as previously mentioned, stimulation of this spot will boost immune response, increase general kidney energy levels and boost will-power levels. Within 10 minutes or so, you may notice an upsurge of enthusiasm and stamina. Whether you actually notice it or not, it will occur. Often you don't notice the shift, which is why the instruction 'take stock of where you are and how you feel' occurs with some regularity throughout the training – to help you to be mindful enough to notice.

11.18 am

Stop pounding abruptly.

Give yourself a moment to appreciate and enjoy the fizzing sensation of energy being activated and released into your system. It may not strike you as deeply significant but try and explain energy intellectually and it quickly goes into the realm of the abstract. However, the fact this gives you an indisputable instant sensation of energy instead, which considering how crucial the ability is to access and be in command of your own energy field in terms of invincibility levels – as soon you'll see – I think makes it deeply significant indeed. So pay attention and appreciate it while it's happening. This is the very current of life itself. You try drumming that up out of nowhere from scratch and you soon realize how clever the Tao really is.

Moving from the one point, slowly raise your torso till upright. Place your palms on your belly. Feel your digestive organs working. Keep breathing. Lengthen your spine. Broaden your hips. Relax. Take stock of where you are and how you feel. Moving from the one point, stand up slowly. Place the book where you can read it standing hands-free.

I'm hoping and assuming that by now you're finding a way to work with the book, as a physical object, harmoniously enough to be practical for training ease as well as enjoyment purposes.

Stand with your feet together, facing due north. Pivot your right foot on the heel 45° to the right to face approximately north-east. Step your left foot directly forward approximately 1 m, facing approximately due north. Bend both knees slightly. Place your body weight 60 per cent on the back leg, 40 per cent on the front leg.

Tuck your sacral bone slightly under at the base of your spine to lengthen your spine from your waist down. Elongate the back of your neck, allowing your chin to drop towards your chest a little, to lengthen your spine from shoulder-level up. Subtly bow that part of your spine between the two, back away from your front.

Place your right hand, palm as if pressing down on a table top flush with your body at waist height, forefinger in line with your navel. Place your left hand, as if pressing with the outer edge of the palm on a wall in front of you, whose base is directly in line and flush with your toes, so your left forefinger is in line with your nose.

Keep breathing. Gaze out gently past your left forefinger, visualizing a laser-like stream of concentrated energy issuing forth into infinity. Relax and soften every muscle group. Let your bones support you and form the shape of your posture but let all your muscles relax and soften, even the front of your thighs.

73

The front of your thighs are the source of your strength and stamina. Using them to support your body weight in this manner, increases access to strength and stamina.

Keep your left knee directly above your left heel. Keep your right knee over the toes of your right foot.

To avoid joint-strain, never extend your front knee past the toes of the front foot.

Keep an eye on the clock. Settle in for a 9-minute stretch of standing there without moving.

In fact, 9 minutes is nothing. Traditionally the pose was held for a minimum of 40 minutes a day – but we don't live in days like that anymore.

Relax your shoulders. Breathe more slowly.

It doesn't matter how slowly – it's all relative – just breathe more slowly.

Place awareness in the one point below the navel. Your only thought is, 'I am standing here like this'.

Which kind of begs a 'you don't say' response – and that's the point. If you can have a laugh with yourself over it, so much the better. I know I've been quite serious up till now, mostly to ensure you got into the groove, but now I'm feeling more confident you are in the groove, I feel it's time to say it's OK to have a laugh while you do the training, as long as you don't become so jokey-jokey that you start getting sloppy with the processes. I think we understand each other.

Keep breathing. As your left arm grows heavier relax your shoulders more.

One of the beauties of Taoist practice is it seems so gentle yet can be so tough and the antidote to that toughness is always simply to relax more. It works as well.

Sensitize yourself to the flow of energy between your left and right hands.

This isn't imaginary. There is energy flow between all phenomena in the universe, including you and I, not to mention between such vast heavenly objects as the Sun and this very planet, so obviously there's energy flow between two things as fundamentally connected as your two hands.

Maintain awareness in the one point below your navel. Sensitize yourself to the energy field, originating in the one point, enveloping your entire body and extending approximately 1 m from the physical periphery all around you: above, below, behind, in front and to the sides.

Again, this isn't just some kind of vague energy theory about your aura. It's not up for discussion. You have an energy field and you are merely being required to sensitize yourself to it.

Keep breathing. As your left arm grows heavier, relax your shoulders more. As your thighs grow tired, relax your hips more. Remain sensitive to the flow of energy between your left hand and right. Maintain awareness in the one point below your navel.

This is asking you to be aware of a few factors simultaneously. You may find yourself hitting one or two of those perfect moments where the whole thing comes into focus but generally you just do the best you can do with it. No one said it was easy.

75

11.27 am

Keep an eye on the clock. Moving slowly and purposefully from the one point, transfer your body weight entirely on to your right foot. Draw your left foot back until your heels are together. Draw your left hand downwards into the table-pressing position, forefinger in line with your navel, matching the position of your right hand.

Pivot your left foot 45° to the left to face approximately north-west. Step the right foot forward approximately 1 m, foot facing approximately due north. Raise your right hand and place it in the wall-pressing position, fore-finger in line with your nose. Distribute your body weight 60 per cent on the left foot, 40 per cent on the right.

Settle in for another 9 minute stretch of standing there without moving. Relax your shoulders. Breathe more slowly. Place awareness in the one point below the navel. Your only thought is, 'I am standing here like this'.

Keep breathing. As your right arm grows heavier relax your shoulders more. Sensitize yourself to the flow of energy between your right hand and left. Maintain awareness in the one point below your navel.

Resensitize yourself to the energy field, originating in the one point, enveloping your entire body and extending approximately 1 m from the physical periphery all around you: above, below, behind, in front and to the sides.

Keep breathing. As your right arm grows heavier relax your shoulders more. As your thighs grow tired, relax your hips more. Remain sensitive to the flow of energy between your right hand and left. Maintain awareness in the one point below your navel.

I should have said already (but didn't want to interrupt the process) that this posture derives from Hsing I – Taoist 'mind-intention boxing' – and is representative of the element of metal, as in blades which slice through the illusion of life to the core truth behind the facade. Standing as you just have for 18 minutes – well done by the way – causes a spontaneous inner slicing away of outworn energy patterns and all associated manifestations – bits of the past that are no longer serving you well enough to hang on to, in other words.

11.36 am

Moving slowly from the one point, draw your right foot backwards until your heels are together. Step around behind and turn so you're facing south.

South because it's good to give your eyes a change of view and because facing south, the magnetic energy streams through in a southerly direction, carrying all the psycho-emotional debris you are about to release, dumping it in the cosmic sea to be cleansed and recycled.

Place your feet shoulder width apart, both feet facing due south. Bend your knees a little. Gently bounce up and down rhythmically and steadily – 1–2 cm either way at first, gradually letting go more into the movement until your entire body is bouncing up and down as if on hefty springs.

Maintain awareness in the one point below your navel. Keep breathing. Keep bouncing. Your only thought is, 'I am bouncing up and down'. Keep an eye on the clock.

(Which might prove tricky in terms of horizontal hold.) This is a gentle way of shaking you up a little to help dislodge any remaining errant stuck bits of personality, hence taking you further into the transpersonal state as opposed to the personal. You are on your way to knowing yourself as pure energy – but maybe I shouldn't have told you that, instead letting you find out for yourself in due course. Maybe it doesn't matter.

11.45 am

Stop bouncing. Still yourself. Settle into the standing posture. Bend your knees. Let your energy settle and your breath normalize. Tuck your pelvis under. Elongate your spine, from the waist down and from the shoulder girdle up.

This is a refinement to the spine-elongation process, now you're more familiar with it in principle, by introducing more specific local reference points around which to do the lengthening. It may help you to see it and feel it better.

Keep breathing. Place awareness in the one point below the navel. Straighten your legs. Remove earplugs. Place palms over ears. Press in to close off the sound. Release to open it up. Close and release alternately 18 times. Adapt to the increase in general volume of sound.

Sit in the chair. Listen to everything. Hear every sound. Identify none of them. Allow sounds without labels or description through your ears into the centre of your brain. Keep breathing. Every sound you hear, tell yourself, 'I have given this all the value it has for me', but desist from naming it.

This is really not easy. It requires slipping into a non-labelling mode, wherein you're entirely receptive and without judgement, as if hearing the entire soundscape in just 2D instead of 3D – in other words as a flat field with no one sound assuming any more importance or dominance than any other. A distant car noise is as important or unimportant as the sound of your stomach gurgling or the birdsong outside your window, if you're lucky. Again, the point is to disarm any formerly concrete version of reality predicated on old opinions.

12.00 pm

Moving from the one point, walk slowly to the bathroom. As your bodyweight falls through your right foot, place awareness in your left hand. As your bodyweight falls through your left foot, place awareness in your right hand. The only thought in your mind is, 'I am walking to the bathroom'.

Empty your bladder and bowels as required. Wash. Become aware of the smells of everything. For each smell, pleasant or otherwise, tell yourself, 'I have given this all the value it has for me'.

Yet again challenging the supremacy of opinions. Perhaps a nice smell is a horrible one and vice versa. Does it even matter? It's all relative here in the world of the world. The only thing that's real in this whole show, contrary to any appearances, is the Tao itself, the inter-connecting, a priori, invisible pattern of supreme consciousness, energy and love, which creates, animates and permeates everything including you and I – which is precisely the realm we are gradually dropping into here with the training.

Change into your outdoor clothes. Moving from the one point, walk slowly to the designated space. Take the pad and pen. Write the following note:

'Excuse me for not talking – I'm doing a 24-hour silent contemplation as part of a personal development training programme – I'll speak to you properly on the phone or next time I see you.'

Remember it's OK to have a laugh – just try and keep it silent and within, one way or another, till 8 pm, even if it turns out you have to act the clown a bit to pull it off. It really doesn't matter.

Fold the note and stow it somewhere safe and easily accessible on your person. If you don't wear a watch, take the alarm clock from the designated space and stow it accessibly and safely somewhere on your person.

If you don't have any specific alarm clock pockets in which to sequester it about your person, take a small shoulder bag.

Turn off lights as appropriate. Put on your outside footwear. Put your keys in your pocket or bag, along with money and phone (in the off position) in case of emergency.

You never know, you might forget. By the way, it's assumed you also take the book with you here.

12.15 pm

Check the time. Leave the building. Walk into the street. Stand still with the street door behind you. Look around you. Take stock of where you are and how you feel.

Take a moment to orientate yourself internally and externally. Do you feel fear, for instance? Do you feel excitement? Maybe a bit of each? Don't try and change it, whatever you feel. Simply feel the air on your face and observe without prejudice.

Keep breathing. Turn left from the front door. Moving from the one point, walk slowly round the block or equivalent in a counter-clockwise direction for 30 minutes. If there is no possibility of walking a complete loop in 30 minutes, walk for 15 minutes and turn back.

The point of walking in a roughly counter-clockwise direction is to encourage the energetic release of the past, as before.

Everything you see, tell yourself, 'I have given this all the value it has for me'.

Just because you're repeating this thought a lot right now doesn't mean you should go numb on it.

Otherwise, your only thought is, 'I am walking along the street'. Keep an eye on the time. Lengthen your spine. Broaden your hips and shoulders. Relax all your muscles.

Now you're meditating in the street.

If you meet anyone you know, show them the note and smile, using facial expression and hand gestures if required but do not speak or make any vocal sound.

12.45 pm

Walk back into your building. Remove your footwear.

Don't rush or go mindless on it. Every action and every part of every action is as important as every other action and every other part of every other action – or unimportant depending on your mood and perspective.

Change into the indoor lounging outfit you've been wearing till now. If required, walk to the bathroom to empty your bladder and bowels and wash. Otherwise, walk directly to the designated space.

Set lighting as required. If you took the alarm clock out walking, replace it. Walk to the kitchen. Prepare a light lunch. As you prepare lunch, the only thought in your mind is, 'I am preparing lunch'.

1.00 pm

Place lunch on a tray. Moving from the one point, walk slowly to the designated space carrying the tray. Sit in the chair. Place the tray on your lap. Place your palms approximately 10 cm above the food.

Think of all the energy involved in getting the food onto your plate. Think of all the people involved in the chain that made it possible. Think of the forces of nature required for the food to exist. Think of how painful it would be to starve to death. Be aware with out guilt that many are doing that actual thing at this precise moment. Be thankful for the food you are about to eat. Let the essence of that gratitude, stream out through your palms into the food.

Eat lunch. Chew each mouthful 18 times. The only thought in your mind is, 'I am eating lunch'. Spend a moment being thankful for the food.

1.30 pm

Stand slowly. Walk to the kitchen carrying the tray. Leave the tray in the kitchen. Walk back to the designated space. Take the pad and pen. Sit in the chair. Relax. Keep breathing. Elongate your spine. Broaden your hips and shoulders. Be aware of the digestive process.

Simply being aware of it helps it along. Wherever you place your awareness, energy and blood will follow.

83

Make a list of all your fears. Don't hold back.

It's not often you give yourself the chance to enumerate your fears. Perhaps you avoid it because you think by mentioning something you give it more power. The purpose of this process, however, is to dispel the power you have already given your fears and put you back in command of your own mind.

List every single fear you have.

From spiders to great heights, from failure and inadequacies to death, from the smallest to the biggest fears you have – list them all.

1.47 pm

Detach the list from the pad. Place the pad and pen down by your side. Read the list. As you read each entry, tell yourself, 'I have given this fear all the negative value it has for me'.

This will free you momentarily and put you back into the present moment. When you think about your fears, what you are doing is projecting into an imaginary future based entirely on your version of the past. Both are merely based on a set of opinions. Remove the negative value you've placed on each of your fears and the energy you were using to hold that fear in place is released into the system to be used positively instead.

Stow the list. Let your arms hang by your side. Make loose fists. Moving from the one point, slowly lower your torso towards your knees until your fists are by the outside of your shins, just below knee-level. Relax your shoulders, elbows and wrists. Pound rhythmically on the fleshiest part of the ridges of muscle, which run down the outsides of your shins just below knee-level.

This is to aid the digestive process, both in terms of the food you've eaten and the information you've been processing. It also stimulates vital kidney energy, which if weak gives rise to an internal atmosphere of fearfulness, but when strong and flowing fills you with the will to override all fears and step forth into the mystery with boldness and aplomb.

Keep an eye on the time.

1.55 pm

Stop pounding suddenly. Place your palms on your belly. Be aware of your digestive process.

Where your awareness goes, your energy follows. Giving your organs and bowels the acknowledgement and respect they deserve, inspires them to work more efficiently on your behalf, thus helping prevent after-meal tiredness while speeding the digestive process.

Stand up. Set the alarm for 2.45 pm. Spread the blanket. Place the 8-cm thick book on the blanket to be used instead of a pillow.

> It's easier to lengthen your spine when your head is raised – mechanically speaking (on account of the S-curve formed by your vertebrae) this allows your lumbar spine to sink more fully and easily into the floor.

Lie down on your back, knees bent, soles flat on the floor, arms by your side. Read the following instructions, from 'apply a fresh blindfold' up to 'remove the blindfold', 3 times carefully and memorize. Apply a fresh blindfold.

> This is to help you go deeper within – yourself, not the floor.

Allow your lower back to sink into the floor. Elongate your spine. Keep breathing. Become aware of all the bones comprising your skeleton. Tell yourself, 'I have given these bones all the value they have for me'. Mentally, become nothing but your bones. Your only thought is, 'I am nothing but these bones'. Remain being nothing but your bones.

> It doesn't get much more basic than this – the skeleton of your being – the core structure around which you hang. Be comfortable with the emptiness of knowing yourself on this fundamental level and all the rest – the flesh, the fluids, the nerves, the energy, the consciousness and the spirit, not to mention all the myriad ways you extend into the external world of the world via your relationships and dialogue with others and your environment – becomes mere bonus to colour the view.

2.45 pm

Remove the blindfold. Lightly place the tip of the forefinger of each hand at the outer corners of your eyes on each side. Stroke ever so softly and slowly along the edge of the bone immediately under each eye until your fingertips are touching the top of your nose on each side by the inner corner of each eye. Stroke softly and slowly along the edge of the bone immediately above each eye until your fingertips are once again at the outside corner of each eye. Repeat this cycle slowly, softly and patiently 18 times. The only thought in your mind is counting the cycles.

This is to wake up the energy and blood flow around your eyes to counter any stagnation caused by the pressure of the blindfold.

Roll to your right, come up onto all fours and stand up slowly, head coming up last. Stand facing north, feet 10 cm apart, legs straight but not totally locked at the knees. Moving from the one point, slowly lower your torso from the hips, as if drawing your chest towards your thighs. Keep elongating your spine. Keep breathing. Relax.

When you've reached the comfortable limit of flexibility in the movement, support your torso by holding your lower legs or feet. Do not bounce. **87**

Bouncing sends alternating mixed messages (relax–contract) to your muscles and may cause them to go into mild trauma. This isn't a test to see how flexible you are in a hamstring stretch. It is a meditative posture in which you have an opportunity of coming up against your previously self-imposed limits and gently penetrating till you dispel them a little more.

Feel the stretch through your hamstrings. Surrender to the sensation. Remain in the stretch for 9 slow inhalation and exhalation cycles. Your only thought is, 'I am hanging forward'.

Your hamstrings are the muscles used to hold you from falling forwards when standing. When over-contracted, this tends to make you hold back from life in general. As well as helping loosen your hamstrings, thus freeing you to move on, elongating your hamstrings opens up your bladder meridian, one of the main energy channels in the body, responsible for carrying the energy from the brain to strengthen all your vital organs and bowels, especially your kidneys, thus energizing you for renewed forward thrust in your life. It also helps reduce lower back pain in most circumstances. However, if you feel any untoward pain or dizziness during this process, stop immediately and consider consulting your GP or medical advisor.

Bend your knees. Moving from the one point, slowly raise your torso from the hips until fully upright, your head coming up last. Walk to the kitchen. Drink water.

As you know, water is the source of all biological life, including yours. While supplies are still relatively abundant, it is a situation unlikely to last for long, so avail yourself as freely as possible of its life-giving qualities. However, it is a mistake to think drinking loads of water will strengthen your kidneys. It will help flush them through but will not actually strengthen them. Everything in moderation.

Walk to the bathroom to empty your bladder and bowels as required.

Use this as a time to commune with the deeper forces of nature running through you. Looking into the toilet bowl, be aware of the intricate system of pipes and sewage treatment responsible for disposing of your waste and give thanks for all the energy, time and work others put in to make this possible for you. Be aware of the consciousness connecting us all and send love out through the S-bend. The Tao, the source of being itself, is everywhere. Use every possible opportunity to feel your connectedness to it.

Walk to the designated space.

3.00 pm

Take the pad and paper. Sit in the chair. Make a list of every single bad habit you have.

Be honest with yourself now. List them all – even the most embarrassing ones. If applicable, include such habits as worrying and beating yourself up. Remember this list is for your eyes only unless you fancy a dose of losing your pride.

When you've finished read through the list.

Do this without judgement. Simply read and observe yourself reading.

After each entry, tell yourself, 'I have given this all the negative value it has for me'. Stow the list.

Watch your mind rebel as it tries in vain to grapple with this concept, yet be perceptive to the brief instant of energy release that will arise in the gap between saying it and when your monkey mind kicks in with its judgements.

Make a list of every single good habit you have.

Include the many relatively small things you may normally overlook or take for granted, like the way you smile at the person in the shop or the way you make a thank you gesture when being given the right of way to cross the road by a motorist – in other words, every small contribution you make to the self-respect and well-being of others as you work, rest and play, along with every other example of a good habit you've got, you can think of.

When you've finished the list, read through it and after each entry, tell yourself, 'I have given this all the positive value it has for me'. Detach the list and stow it.

Feeling a bit better?

3.20 pm

Place the pen and pad on the floor by your side. Stand up.

I know – sit down, stand up – it's starting to become a joke, but it's not a joke. Stay with it – it'll be worth it.

Put in a new pair of earplugs or cotton wool equivalent. Stand facing south with your feet shoulder width apart, both feet facing due south. Bend your legs a bit. Listen within to the beat of your heart. From the one point below the navel, start to sway your hips in time with the beat. Allow the movement to slowly spread throughout your body until every part is fully animated in dance. Now let the dance animate you. The only thought in your mind is, 'I am fully animated in dance'. Keep an eye on the clock.

3.30 pm

Stop suddenly and freeze in whichever position you're in. Hold the position. Keep breathing. Count 3 slow cycles of inhalation and exhalation. Realign your posture till standing perfectly straight again.

That might have been the deepest dance you've ever done.

Set the alarm to go off at 4.10 pm. Spread the blanket.

You need a rest.

Place the book for use as a pillow.

Get ready. This is an important bit coming up.

Lie down on the blanket with the book under your head, facing up, knees bent, soles flat on the floor, arms by your sides. Read the following instructions carefully 3 times and memorize from, 'close your eyes', till, 'open your eyes'.

Close your eyes. Draw your consciousness back into the centre of your brain. Keep breathing. Let your thoughts drift.

This is freefall – go with it. If you feel panic coming on – now or anytime in your life – breathe more slowly and try scooping the loop, drawing energy up the rear of your backbone on the in-breath and down the front of your backbone on the out-breath. This will strengthen your spirit and keep you moving forwards into the mystery.

4.10 pm

Open your eyes. Lightly place the tip of the forefinger of each hand at the outer corners of your eyes on each side. Stroke ever so softly and slowly along the edge of the bone immediately under each eye until your fingertips are touching the top of your nose on each side by the inner corner of each eye. Stroke softly and slowly along the edge of the bone immediately above each eye until your fingertips are once again at the outside corner of each eye. Repeat this cycle slowly, softly and patiently 18 times. The only thought in your mind is counting the cycles.

You're doing this now because you are about to be required to do a bit of staring and your eyes need to be relaxed for it.

Roll to your left. Go onto all fours. Stand up slowly. Reset the alarm to go off at 4.30 pm. Take the mirror.

This is a good one – immensely powerful, in fact. If you ever wanted proof that your very existence as you've come to know yourself, is entirely a matter of opinion, here it is.

Sit in the chair. Relax your shoulders. Keep breathing. Hold the mirror in front of you. Let your gaze fall on the reflection of your own eyes. Stare into your eyes. Allow your facial features to blur and distort. Keep staring into your own eyes.

It's quite likely here that an entire melange of rushing images will assail your gaze – versions of your face as an old woman, an old man, a crone, a wizard, a princess, a prince, a dissolute fool, a sage, a profligate knave, a wise scholar, a Greek goddess, a Taoist Golden Immortal, a Native American medicine woman, a Tibetan lama, a demon, an angel – maybe even the supreme being itself – all flashing by as various dimensions and depths of your psyche come to the fore to reveal themselves. Or, as some would say, you remember all your past lives.

Allow your face to disappear altogether.

As it will just about now. Don't be afraid.

Keep breathing. Every time your facial features reform, relax, detach, stare into your eyes and allow them to dissolve and disappear again. Your only thought is, 'I have disappeared'.

93

4.30 pm

Put the mirror down carefully.

This, even though you've disappeared, is called trans-dimensional multitasking.

Moving from the one point, stand up. Walk slowly into the kitchen. Make a hot drink – jasmine tea, green tea or plain boiled water. Take the drink into the designated space.

I'm tempted to say, '... or take it wherever you like – it's your tea', but we either take this seriously and gain the full effect or we don't.

Sit down. Drink it slowly. Your only thought is, 'I am drinking this slowly'. Feel the effects of the warm fluid passing through your stomach and gastrointestinal tract. Stand up. Take the cup back into the kitchen. Wash the plates from lunchtime or rinse and place in dishwasher. As you do, your only thought is, 'I'm cleaning the crockery'.

You think I'm joking now, don't you. Actually, I'm really not. I'm being serious. There are few things worse than a sink full of dirty dishes when you are trying to keep a clear head. That's just simple feng shui.

Walk to the bathroom. Remove earplugs. Empty your bladder and bowels as required. Wash. Massage your ears – all surfaces, cracks and crevices – gently but thoroughly between fingers and thumbs until they grow hot.

This wakes up what's called your 'ancestral energy', or, if you like, the energy of your DNA and stimulates its flow throughout your system. If you look at your ear, you'll notice that as well as looking like a kidney, it also bears a strong resemblance to a baby in the womb, upside down in foetal position, its head where your lobe is and so on. This baby is you, as you were in the pre-natal state – hence it is the deepest or near-deepest part of you, here in this current earth-plane incarnation. As each sector of the ear is stimulated, the corresponding sector of the body receives a healing message – you have just been healed, thank you – that sort of thing. For this reason, ear massage is considered a boon to longevity.

Reinsert earplugs. Walk to designated space.

4.50 pm

Take the pen and pad. Sit in the chair. Relax.
You're not at school.

Keep breathing. Make a list of everything in your life you'd like to leave behind if only you could.
Such as the insane grip that your internalized version of teachers at school still have on you and the way you think and act – and that's just one example.

Don't hold back. List every facet of your being that no longer serves you, every complex that still hangs you up, every fear pattern that prevents you being free, every situation that holds you back, every relationship that impedes your full expression of love, every obstacle to you reaching full potential in this life. Take your time.

This is a big one. Don't rush it. take your time. This should be immensely therapeutic and only needs to be seen by anyone you may happen to mention in the list, if you actually want them to – consciously or unconsciously.

Keep an eye on the clock.

I see no paradox in this – or if there is, it's a paradox worthy of accommodating. Take all the time you want until 5.10 pm.

5.10 pm

Read through the list. After each entry, tell yourself, 'I am willing to let this dissolve now'. Note any fear or resistance arising as a physical sensation of tightness in the chest, belly or back of the neck.

You are not telling it or pleading with it to dissolve, you're merely stating that you're willing for it to dissolve if it wants to – in other words, you're willing to release any grip you may hitherto have been inadvertently exerting to hold it in place. And you can't be any fairer than that.

Tell yourself, 'I have given this the negative value it has for me'. Breathe slowly. Relax your chest, belly and the back of your neck.

Turn an obstacle into a neutral phenomenon and the next thing you know it's your ally. You don't need to trust me on that one. Find out for yourself.

Stow the list. Moving from the one point, stand up slowly. Stand, feet together, arms by your sides, palms facing in touching outsides of thighs, facing approximately due north. Bend your knees slightly. Tuck your sacral bone at the base of your spine, under a bit, to elongate your spine from waist-level down. Drop your chin slightly and soften the back of your neck, to elongate your spine from shoulder-level up.

I expect that by now you're starting to welcome this, what we call in the trade 'the drop'. After a while it starts to grow extremely reassuring in the midst of the storm, which is good because what follows if done correctly is a powerful move and requires full presence of mind. The point is that you have to empty fully before you have the space and capacity to take on what amounts to the miracle of the new, including you being invincible. To be invincible you first have to not exist in the first place so there's nothing to destroy. It's not easy – if you're doing it properly and bringing yourself fully to bear on what you're doing – but it's simple as pie.

Moving from the one point, slowly raise your arms sideways to shoulder-height, to form a 'T' shape with your palms facing the floor.

This is a classic white crane chi kung move and as well as its mystical significance and use in terms of helping you dumping the past, it is extremely good for the health of your armpits and all the important blood vessels running through them, as well as the nerves of your brachial plexus, not to mention the tops of your lungs.

Relax your neck. Relax your shoulders. Rotate your arms at the shoulder joints slightly till your palms are angled to face behind you. Keep breathing. Extend your shoulder-tips away from your spine. Extend your elbows away from your shoulders. Extend your wrists away from your elbows. Extend your knuckles away from your wrists. But do not lock your elbows, wrists or knuckles. Let your skeleton make the shape of the posture.

Relax and soften all your muscles. As your arms grow tired, relax your shoulders more. Keep an eye on the clock. Keep breathing. Think of the contents of all the lists you've made during the past 20 hours and 47 minutes or so.

The contents of these lists, needless to point out, constitute pretty much your entire version of who you've been till now. That's probably quite a steamy old combo.

Imagine all that content mixed together and transformed into gaseous form in your upper abdomen.

I hesitate to suggest colouring it and if so whether to colour it dull or bright – that's for you to decide, though personally, if it was me (which it often is) I'd colour it dull pretty much the way white t-shirts come grey out after you wash them with the wrong things.

With each successive exhalation, feel this gas rising progressively into your chest, across into your shoulders, down your arms and being expelled through the centre of each palm, thence to disperse in the air behind you.

Once released, this 'gas' will be naturally transformed into neutral then positive energy to be used more effectively elsewhere – recycled in other words.

Repeat this for the length of 6 cycles of inhalation and exhalation.

Numerologically speaking, the number 6 represents and evokes the power of reduction, as opposed to 9, which represents the power of increase.

Moving from the one point, slowly rotate your arms back the other way, till your palms are angled to face the floor again. Slowly lower your arms to your sides. Notice the sensation of increased circulation across your chest and upper back.

Being so intimately connected to pride, your chest – and to some extent upper abdomen – is where you house a lot of that fragile complex web you've hitherto regarded as yourself. Through holding the posture with sensitivity to what's going on across your chest, you undo the shape you were holding yourself in, along with all the energy required to help you do that – this in order that you may be free of the burden and ready to rebuild with a (far) more stable, flexible and resilient structure. It should also be said that the strengthening effect of the move, helps increase your emotional stability in general – which makes sense if you consider that it's your upper abdomen and chest where you feel most of your emotions.

Keep breathing. Take stock of where you are and how you feel.

Incidentally, by now, if you happen to be doing the training with a partner, friend or – if bathroom logistics permit – friends, you'll probably be experiencing a marked increase in telepathic communication between you. Likewise if doing it solo, an increase in telepathy with others in absentia, something you'll probably verify when you check your messages at the end of the training or whenever you feel appropriate (as long as you don't start returning them before the training's done – other than in an emergency, of course).

5.35 pm

Arrange your blanket on the floor. Lie down on your back, knees bent, soles of your feet flat on the floor. Allow your lower back to broaden and sink into the floor. Keep breathing. Place your arms by your sides. Moving from the one point 6 cm below your navel, slowly raise your torso off the floor until you feel the muscles in your belly contract. Keep your lower back fully sunk into the floor. Keep breathing. Relax all muscle groups not being actively used in the raising motion, especially the back of your neck. Hold the posture. Breathe slowly. Count 36 cycles of inhalation and exhalation.

This is upping the ante on this morning's Taoist sit-up session, by asking you to meditate for twice as long in the posture. It's imperative you relax throughout. If you get the trembles, relax into it more and enjoy them – trembles are merely the result of trapped energy being released. One Hsing I master, Divine Crushing Fist, I think it was, correct me if I'm wrong, used to stand perfectly still before commencing practice of the forms – and would stand there until his body started trembling. He would then proceed to get off on that for a good few minutes and only then start his moves. Trembling freely is a good thing in the right place at the right time.

Lower your torso slowly till your entire back is lying flat again. Let your lower back sink into the floor. Lengthen your spine. Relax everything. Keep breathing. Count 3 cycles of inhalation and exhalation. Repeat the entire process of raising and lowering the torso 9 times.

This is serious stuff now. It must be done in a fully relaxed manner to avoid injury or strain. On the other hand, the benefits of increasing your core strength, specifically around the one point, are massive.

Place your palms on your belly. Mentally repeat the word 'strength' 9 times. Turn onto your front. Stretch your legs out straight behind you, feet together. Place your palms on the floor, just to the outside of your shoulders. Lengthen your spine, especially the back of your neck. Keep breathing. Pull your buttocks and the muscles of your lower back inwards towards the spine.

Moving from the one point below your navel, slowly raise your torso approximately 10 cm from the floor. Maintain the inward pull of the buttocks and lower back muscles. Relax all other muscle groups, especially at the back of the neck. Breathe more slowly. Count 18 cycles of inhalation and exhalation. Lower your torso slowly to the floor. Repeat the sequence 3 times through.

> Likewise, this is upping this morning's ante by double. Again it's more than crucial that you remain fully relaxed and sensitive to what's going in internally throughout to avoid injury or strain. On the other hand, the increase in strength this gives your lumbar spine region – and by extension to your very psycho-physical foundation – is what you're doing this one for, so don't hold back, if you'll excuse the pun.

Focusing awareness on your buttocks and lower back, mentally repeat the word 'strength' 9 times. Roll to your right and lie on your back. Bend your legs at the knees. Place your soles flat on the floor, legs together.

> Here comes the Taoist twist stretch again. It's good to give your body the same message a few times a day. The more you do it, the more Monkey relaxes and goes with it, the easier it gets for all concerned.

101

Stretch your arms out to the sides perpendicular to your torso to form a 'T'. Turn your head to face your right hand. Turning from the one point below your navel, let your legs slowly fall over to the left until your left knee is on the floor. Keep breathing. Feel the stretch across your torso. Enjoy feeling the stretch through your hips. Resist resisting it. Breathe more slowly. Count 18 cycles of inhalation and exhalation.

Moving from the one point below your navel, slowly draw your legs straight and turn your head till gazing up at the ceiling. Turn your head to face your left hand. Turning from the one point below your navel, let your legs slowly fall over to the right until your right knee is on the floor. Keep breathing. Feel the stretch across your torso. Breathe more slowly. Count 9 cycles of inhalation and exhalation. Moving from the one point below your navel, slowly draw your legs straight and turn your head till gazing up at the ceiling. Place both palms on your chest. Mentally repeat the word 'strength' 9 times.

The stronger and more open your chest feels, the more love you can process – and love is the currency you thrive on. And in any case it feels magnificent when you stand up, all opened up like that – nice and juicy with the chi flowing through your shoulders. More importantly at this stage – and I should have mentioned it earlier but you can't cram it all in at once – this opening across the upper chest helps you shed years of stagnant emotional upset and wounded pride as the energy and corresponding holding pattern in the muscles, is released.

Roll to your left. Come onto all fours. Let your head hang down. Relax the back of your neck. Keep breathing. Keep an eye on the clock. Moving from the one point, slowly sit back on your heels. If this is impossible or extremely uncomfortable, sit in the chair and push your buttocks well back in the seat. Slowly lower your chest towards your knees. Place your palms flat on the floor out in front of you, in line with your shoulders. Use your arms to support you and let your chest slowly drop closer to your knees – all the way down if you can but don't force it. Do not bounce.

Bouncing in a stretch is a sign of impatience and is essentially treating your body more disrespectfully than it deserves by giving your muscles mixed messages – lengthen, shorten, lengthen, shorten – till they don't know what to do and go into freeze mode and you end up injured. So don't bounce in a stretch.

Relax your hips.

This may sound like nothing so special but relaxed hips are key to a healthy sex life, being sexy, being self-accepting and being generally in the groove of life rather than being square. Relaxed hips make your reality more curvy – and we like curves because that's the way nature shapes itself. It's only the rational aspect of the monkey mind that wants everything to be in straight lines. There are no straight lines as it turns out, seeing as this is a curved universe. Every straight line eventually curls back on itself. The Taoist way is to see the curve in every straight line. So, to cut a long story short, relax your hips. **103**

Broaden across your hips and lower back. Sensitize yourself to the energy flowing between your sacral bone at the base of your spine and your upper brainstem at the top of your spine inside your skull, just under the central brain region. Keep breathing. Draw your consciousness back into the centre of your brain, just above the top of your upper brainstem. Keep breathing. Feel the in-breath travel from your sacrum up the rear of your spine to the top of your brain. Feel the out-breath travel from the top of your brain down the front of your spine into your pelvic floor. Watch this all happening from the centre of your brain.

There you have the nub of Taoist inner spiritual training in a nutshell. It is this very loop which delineates the shape, so to speak, of your spirit and helps give it energetic substance, so that even when you drop your body for good, your consciousness won't be scattered. How much more invincible, therefore, when just used in everyday mortal life.

6.25 pm

Moving from the one point, push your buttocks back and down and slowly raise your torso till you're sitting straight, arms hanging by your sides. Keep watching yourself doing all this from the centre of your brain.

Gradually you become more used to drawing your consciousness back into a single point like this, so that by the time you've done the training, it's habitual, at which point, you're gazing at the world through the eyes of the spirit and that's when the magic really starts happening in your life.

Keep breathing. Maintain awareness in the one point below your navel.

You start to get the sense that the one point is inextricably connected to and part of the same unit as the central brain vantage point, so that as you look out from there, your very looking is supported by the energy of the one point.

According to the inner architecture of Taoist internal alchemy practice, you have three *tan tien* or fields of heaven within your body. The lowest is your one point below the navel. Through this, heaven powers your movements in the world of the world – all your actions and deeds. The next one, is bang in the middle of your chest – your heart centre. Through this, heaven loves you and causes that love to pour out to others through you. The uppermost is in the dead centre of your brain – the 'cave of your original spirit'. Through this, heaven enlightens you and causes your light to shine forth and illuminate others through you. When I say heaven, I mean the Tao but it doesn't matter what you call it. You can't describe it however hard you try. And why try in the first place?

Place your palms on the floor in front of you and using them as support, slowly stand. Walk to the bathroom. Empty your bladder and bowels as required. Wash. Give yourself a nod in the bathroom mirror.

You need all the encouragement you can get now – always, in fact, but now especially because you are gradually winding up to the climax of the self-deconstruction process and it's going to get a bit more adventurous very shortly.

Walk to the kitchen. Prepare a simple dinner, requiring only 28 minutes preparation time or less, which you can then leave for 35 minutes while you shower or bathe, and which will then be ready to eat at 7.30. Your only thought is, 'I am preparing dinner'.

6.55 pm

Moving from the one point below your navel, walk slowly to the bathroom. Remove earplugs. Place palms over the ears. Open and close the ears by alternately pressing and releasing the palms, 18 times.

Feel the force of subtle pressure as the energy is shunted down from your ears into your kidney region.

Empty your bladder and bowels as required. Take a shower or bath. Keep an eye on the clock. Wash your body from the head down. As you wash your body, tell yourself, 'I'm cleansing myself of everything on all the lists I've written, including even the good points'. Tell yourself, 'I'm cleansing myself of the past. I am ready to take on the new now'.

This may seem like labouring the point but when you consider all the years it took to build up that history, it makes sense that you'll have to do a fair amount of flushing before you properly dislodge it. There's nothing superstitious about it. In any case, this is something in future you'll want to continue to prevent fresh build-up, so the more of a habit you get into about it now, the better.

This represents a major moment in the training – introducing the seed of the idea of taking on the new. Till now the focus has been solely on deconstruction. Now the first glimmer of reconstruction appears, just as the deconstruction process nears its apex – as is the way with yin transforming into yang.

7.15 pm

Get out of the shower or bath. Dry off. Attend to all the essential grooming moves necessary for a relatively social evening.

Notice any fear this provokes. Don't do anything to change or smother it. Simply observe yourself.

Keep breathing. Relax. Watch yourself doing all this from the centre of your brain. Looking at your reflection in the mirror, tell yourself, 'I have given what I see here all the value it has for me'.

Are you feeling the liberating effect of that yet?

Put on your social, going-out outfit.

7.30 pm

Moving from the one point, walk slowly to the kitchen. Place the prepared meal on a tray. Carry the tray into the designated space. Sit in the chair. Place the tray on your lap.

Be careful not to spill any on your going-out outfit. Maybe you should wear a napkin.

Place your palms approximately 10 cm above the food. Think of all the energy involved in getting the food onto your plate. Think of all the people involved in the chain that made it possible. Think of the forces of nature **107** required for the food to exist. Think of how painful it is to starve. Be thankful for the food you are about to eat. Let the essence of that gratitude, stream out through your palms into the food. Eat dinner. Chew each mouthful 18 times. The only thought in your mind is, 'I am eating dinner'.

Remain in the present moment and resist the compulsion to project forward into the future. You're doing what you're doing and that's all there is.

When you've finished, stand up slowly. Moving from the one point, walk slowly to the kitchen. Place the tray down.

7.55 pm

Walk to the designated space. Sit down. Place your palms on your belly. Sensitize yourself to the digestive process. Be thankful for the food that sustains you. Breathe in and out slowly 3 times. Sighing vocally on the out-breath, slide your voice down from falsetto to bass.

This will settle your stomach and calm your nerves.

Stand facing north, feet together, arms by your sides. Keep breathing. Watch yourself doing it from the centre of your brain. Slowly bend your knees a little. Tuck in your sacral bone. Lengthen your spine from waist-level down. Drop your chin and soften the back of your neck. Place your hands, palms facing up, at waist height in front of you, as if holding a large bowl, forefingers in line with the one point. Maintain enough space in each armpit to fit a small apple.

Sensitize yourself to the energy flowing along your spine from the sacral bone at the base to the upper brainstem. Sensitize yourself to the energy flowing between your hands. Sensitize yourself to the energy field emanating from the one point below your navel and surrounding you up to a distance of 3 m from your physical periphery: above, below, behind, before and to the sides of you. Keep breathing. Watch yourself doing it all from the centre of your brain.

This is to introduce and activate a protective sheath of energy around you, to keep you safe in your meditative state out in the world. Martial arts training was initially introduced to the monasteries for this very reason – to keep the seeker safe on the path. Eventually it becomes instinctual and automatic to do it every time you are about to leave wherever you are and pretty much all the rest of the time too. This is a major component of invincibility. At first you have to take it on in good faith but you'll no doubt have many instances of proof to verify its veracity as time goes by.

109

8.00 pm

Say out loud 6 times, 'This energy protects me'.

This, because as you ordain it, so it will be.

Slowly raise your palms to chest height. Make a fist in your right hand, palm-side facing your chest. Place your left palm on the outside of your right fist to shield it.

This is a traditional Taoist martial arts bow, politely shielding your potential power as you humble yourself in the face of the Tao. Changing from the prayer position at this point is to signify that there is now substance within, the kernel of the invincible self, capable of great shows of personal power, the potential of which it humbly and modestly shields from public view.

Bow to the north. Bow to the east. Bow to the south. Bow to the west. Turn off the lights as required. Take your keys, money, phone (which you should leave in the 'off' position to use only in case of emergencies), this book and anything else required for a low-key social occasion.

8.10 pm

Leave the building. Take stock of where you are and how you feel.

It's important to keep checking in with yourself like this. No judgement is required on what you find. No changing of the state – merely observation and noticing.

If you are doing the training accompanied, speak to your fellow partici-pants if you feel the need at this point. Otherwise, ideally all participants should separate at this point for maximum impact. If that's impossible, im-provise as best you can to engender the same effect.

Strangely enough, after 24-hours silence during which you have all but learned total telepathy, talking for the sake of it becomes less of an urgent priority – and seeing as at least 99 per cent of what we say comprises mere talk for the sake of making sound, it's quite likely you and anyone involved will find it easier to remain mostly silent. Imagine how still everything would be if we were all like that. Imagine the pubs, bars and restaurants. It really would be rather weird wouldn't it? I guess that's why we all talk so much all the time – giving way to Monkey. But that's alright, as long as you don't get lost and become the monkey yourself. I should say at this point that I absolutely adore monkeys and feel we have much to learn from them in terms of movement and relaxation. Indeed, I'm a bit of a dab hand at the monkey style of Hsing I boxing myself. But I draw a distinction between the monkey species and Monkey specifically. Just so you know I'm not a rabid monkey-hater.

Act naturally.

Acting naturally is a paradox in itself. If you're being natural you're not acting and if you acting you're not being natural. But that's OK. On some level, unless you're fully realized and have vanished alto-gether to become the Tao itself, it's all an act. The best way to achieve the natural state is to focus on what's occurring within rather than on how you appear. It's all in the breathing and letting go.

Keep breathing. Relax. Constantly moving from the one point now, go somewhere unfamiliar in the vicinity or within a short drive, where you'll be required, to some extent, to talk to and interact with others in a social environment, where there'll be a bit of noise and colour for approximately one hour. There is no need to look at any clocks, wristwatches or other timepieces. Let your unconscious mind keep track of the time for you. The chosen venue could be a bar, pub or club, preferably somewhere you never or rarely frequent and wouldn't normally think of frequenting.

This is intended to provoke a certain level of fear in order to wake you up even more. An interlude during which you can experience yourself in the neutral tipping point between deconstructed and reconstructed.

As you walk in, tell yourself you are nothing but energy, vibrating at sufficient frequency to hold your physical form in shape.

This will accentuate your altered state, hence why it's so important to remain centred by maintaining awareness in the one point as you move about and interact. What's going on inside you is about to become this evening's entertainment. What's going on around you is merely the scenery and supporting cast doing their thing to turn it into something special rather than just a one-man show.

Keep repeating this to yourself: 'I am nothing but energy, vibrating at sufficient frequency to hold this physical form in shape'. Let your gaze fall discreetly on each of the people present, one by one. Take your time. As your gaze falls on each person, tell yourself, they are nothing but energy, vibrating at sufficient frequency to hold their physical form in shape.

Try not to look too intense or glazy-eyed as you do this. Best to keep your face relaxed.

Engage in whatever commerce is required in observing appropriate conventional protocol. If this requires buying a drink, it's recommended to keep it alcohol free.

It's not that there's anything particularly wrong with the warming effects of alcohol but the more you dampen the raw emotions the less impact the process will have.

If this could cause undue stress, keep it to one glass of something light.

This next instruction is inserted to bring you into a heightened state with your adrenalin pumping by which you can gauge without prejudice your centring abilities learned so far.

Introduce yourself to at least one person you don't know, preferably the one you would normally be most scared to.

This was never necessarily going to be easy. Breathe, feel the fear, override the fear and do it.

As you approach them, remind yourself, they are nothing but energy, vibrating at sufficient frequency to hold their physical form in shape. Assure them warmly that you're not an oddball or cult member.

Remember to take enough breath in to support your words as you speak. Remember to keep some awareness in the one point to centre you. Keep breathing. Don't hold your breath. You'll no doubt feel a bit stupid as this is all about losing your pride but stupid is only stupid so don't let it hamper your enjoyment. Embarrassment is the closest thing to bliss, in terms of altered states.

Explain you're doing personal development training and are required to talk to someone you don't know, whom you'd normally be too afraid to approach.

Do this self-deprecatingly and humbly, yet with humour, warmth and respect, lest you inadvertently trigger their defences and give rise to hostility.

Show them the book. Point to this instruction. Have a laugh together. If the conversation goes no further, of its own accord, take your leave warmly and politely. If it goes further, let it go where it wants but remember to breathe and relax throughout. Keep checking the time on your internal clock. Watch yourself doing it all from the centre of your brain. Relax. Keep breathing. Keep repeating to yourself, 'I am nothing but energy, vibrating at sufficient frequency to hold this physical form in shape'. If you enjoyed that so much you'd like to repeat it, do so with the second most scary-looking person there and so on.

Obviously it's impossible to instruct precisely at this point as there are way too many variables to consider. It's all down to improvisation at this point really. The ability to improvise is also a crucial component of invincibility.

9.45 pm

Go home (or to the training venue).

10.00 pm

Check the time. Change from your social outfit into the brighter of the two outfits.

The brighter of the two outfits is now chosen to signify the celebratory mode of taking on the new.

Say out loud, 'I'm willing to see my life get brighter now'. Walk to the bathroom. Empty your bladder and bowels as required. Wash. Looking in the mirror, your only question is, 'Who am I?'

And don't try answering it. You'll never come up with a definitive answer and it really doesn't matter anyway as long as you don't lose your mobile phone and all your numbers if you haven't copied your SIM card because that's a proper drag whoever you are or aren't.

10.10 pm

Moving from the one point below your navel, walk slowly to the kitchen. Drink water. As you do, your only thought is, 'I am drinking water'. Be thankful for the water.

Never take the essentials for granted.

Wash up the dinner dishes or rinse and place in the dishwasher.

10.20 pm

Moving from the one point below your navel, walk slowly to the designated space. Set the lighting. Spread the blanket on the floor. Lie down (without the book), knees bent, soles of the feet flat on the floor, arms by your sides. Even if you feel happy, start moaning out loud. Even if you have nothing in the entire universe to moan about, simply method-act your way into it. Use your whole body to express the emotion. If your moan wants to turn into a full-blown groan, let it.

Moan for all the pain you've ever felt. Moan for all the times you deluded yourself you weren't enough. Moan for all the times you excluded yourself from the party. Moan for all the times you mistakenly thought you were all alone. Moan for all the times you were hard on yourself for no reason. Moan for all the things you regret. Moan for all the things you fear. Moan for all the existential angst you've ever felt. Moan for the sake of moaning.

(How often do you get the chance, after all?)

Moan for the suffering of all humankind. Moan for the suffering of all life. Let it come, let it come. Moan your heart out.

If this triggered you properly you may well be feeling tearful and even have the urge to weep – hence the box of tissues. On no account hold back.

10.35 pm

Stop moaning. Wipe your eyes if required. Relax your body. Lie still.

Doesn't that feel good?

If you want to laugh, laugh. If you want to cry, cry. Either way, keep breathing. Watch yourself doing it from deep inside the centre of your brain. Remind yourself, 'I am nothing but energy, vibrating at sufficient frequency to hold this physical form in shape'. Orientate yourself around the idea that as nothing but energy, vibrating at sufficient frequency to hold your physical form in shape, you are free and able to inform that energy with any qualities you see fit. Tell yourself, '... and that's precisely what I'm going to do tomorrow'.

Because that's precisely what you are going to do, so no self-delusion there.

10.55 pm

Moving from the one point, roll to your left onto all fours. Let your head hang down. Soften the back of your neck. Keep breathing. Slowly stand up. Face approximately due north. Stand with feet at shoulder-width, arms hanging by your sides. Bend your knees slightly. Tuck your sacral bone under slightly. Lengthen your spine from waist-level down. Drop your chin and soften the back of your neck. Lengthen your spine from shoulder-level up. Keep breathing. Moving from the one point, rotate your forearms till your palms face forward. Bend at the elbows slightly. Raise your arms and open them outwards in a wide-embrace position.

Be expansive about this – don't be mean. You are about to welcome and embrace something huge – your new good – and the manner in which you welcome it will determine the tone of how it treats you in return.

Relax your shoulders. Keep breathing. Visualize all the new that is coming to you now – the mystery of the unknown – as a brightly coloured gaseous presence with an appealing scent, swirling about with considerable force in front of you. In the spirit of true hospitality, welcome it into your life. Using the inhalation as a mental trigger, draw it in through the centre of each palm, along each arm, through each shoulder, down through your chest and into your belly.

This style of breathing visualization is central to Taoist martial arts and mental conditioning practice – drawing or expelling a force, imbued with whichever qualities you choose to ascribe it. Like King Canute trying to turn back the waves – except for real.

Repeat 9 full inhalation–exhalation cycles, progressively welcoming the new more and more with each cycle.

The 9 here is to impart extra poke to the process.

As your arms grow tired, relax your shoulders more. Out loud, say, 'It's all new from here'.

Say this cheerfully. All change is good, if you believe it to be and are willing to let it be, come what may. So face your new good with courage.

Lower your arms slowly, until down by your sides. Rotate your forearms back till your palms face in. Relax your elbows. Straighten your legs. Place your feet together. Slowly swing both arms forward and raise to chest-level. Make a fist in your right hand. Place your left palm over your right fist to shield it. Bow to the north. Turn and bow to the east. Turn and bow to the south. Turn and bow to the west. Turn off lights as required.

This is to pay your respects and humble yourself before the Tao in all its guises and directions. You either make yourself subservient to and follow the flow of the Tao, The Great Way, or to the will, agenda and expectations of other people – the lesser way. There is nothing in between.

11.15 pm

Moving from the one point, walk to the kitchen. Drink water and prepare any bedtime drinks or snacks. Take them to your sleeping place.

This is really not meant to be patronizing on the part of the training – merely compassionate and thoughtful.

119

**Walk to the bathroom. Undress. Empty your bladder and bowels as re-
quired. Wash and take care of the essentials. Put on nightwear.**
I can imagine you in your pyjamas even as we speak.

11.30 pm

Walk to your sleeping place.
I call it your sleeping place because you may be using the designated
space to double up, in which case, as soon as you've done your bows,
consider it undesignated and therefore appropriate for sleeping in
until next instructed to walk to the designated space. It's impossible
to predict all contingencies in the instructions but every care as
is humanly possible has been taken to keep them as realistic for a
64-hour non-stop mediation and mindfulness session, so you may
rest assured.

**Set the alarm to go off at 8.30 am. Get into bed. Lie back against the pillows,
facing up. Keep breathing. Take stock of where you are and how you feel.**
I'd expect you to be feeling some kind of shift occurring by now, this
many hours in to what must surely be – assuming you've been following the instructions relatively to the letter– one of the most profound
repositioning process of your life so far, meditatively speaking.

Decelerate your breathing.
The slower your breathing, the calmer your mind.

Tell yourself, 'I now sleep deeply through the night and remain conscious as I dream and awake 6 full minutes before the alarm rings, feeling refreshed, rejuvenated, revitalized and ready for anything'. Read the following instructions 3 times carefully from, 'place the book down', up to, 'pick up the book and open it', and memorize. Mark your place in the book.

Place the book down. Turn off the light. Close your eyes. Sink your consciousness back into the centre of your brain. As if you had a third eye in the centre of your forehead, gaze out through it at the darkened room. Just before falling fully asleep, turn onto your right side.

> The reason for this is to enable your blood to flow more freely towards your liver, which lies on the right side below your ribs, where it will be purified as you sleep. Sleeping on your left side encourages the blood to flow to your heart instead, which being responsible for the quality of your dreams tends to give rise to crazy nightmares and other such disturbing nocturnal events when overloaded.

> Sleep well. Angels on your pillow.

sunday (or third day of training)

reconstruction: the reharnessing process

Not like an ox – but in the yogic sense (the Sanskrit word apparently has the same root as the English word 'yoke') of yoking your local self, along with your chattering monkey mind, to the spirit or deeper guiding intelligence within.

8.24 am

Wake up.

Unless of course you already have, in which case, good morning.

Take stock of where you are and how you feel.

I hope you'll remember the following instruction from the night before or there could turn out to be a bit of a hiatus around this point.

Pick the book up and open it.

Good. Are you ready for this?

Tell yourself, 'I choose to enjoy this day come what may', 6 times.

> If you can grab your mind of an early morning, before it's fully had time to wake itself up, you can most effectively implant ideas that will lodge in your unconscious and thus change the tone of the day completely.

Lightly place the tip of the forefinger of each hand at the outer corners of your eyes on each side. Stroke ever so softly and slowly along the edge of the bone immediately under each eye until your fingertips are touching the top of your nose on each side by the inner corner of each eye. Stroke softly and slowly along the edge of the bone immediately above each eye until your fingertips are once again at the outside corner of each eye. Repeat this cycle slowly, softly and patiently 18 times. The only thought in your mind is counting the cycles.

> The simple act of counting to the exclusion of most other thoughts can be extremely focusing and stilling for the mind.

8.30 am

Rolling to one side or the other, slowly get out of bed. Moving your body from the one point 6 cm below your navel, walk slowly to the bathroom. The only thought in your mind is, 'I'm walking slowly to the bathroom'. Empty your bladder and bowels as required. Greet yourself in the mirror. Say hello. Wash, shower and take care of all the essentials. Dry off and put on the brighter of the two indoor lounging outfits again.

9.30 am

Moving from the one point 6 cm below your navel, walk slowly to the kitchen. The only thoughts in your mind are 'I am walking slowly to the kitchen', and 'I have given this all the value it has for me', in respect of whatever your gaze falls upon. Make hot and cold beverages as required and drink.

9.45 am

Set the alarm in the kitchen for 10.17 am. Do whatever you like till the alarm rings. Do not eat. Do not leave the house. Do not use the phone (except in emergencies). Do not turn on the TV, radio or computer. Do not play any electronic games. Your only thought is, 'I am now doing whatever I like'.

This should be interesting for you. Simply observe yourself pacing about and figuring out what to do with yourself, with your options so limited. That's the point of this particular – what would you call it – anti-process.

10.17 am

Walk into the designated space. Stand with feet together facing approximately due north. Place hands together in 'prayer' position. Bow to the north. Turn and bow to the east. Turn and bow to the south. Turn and bow to the west.

Pay your respects to the Tao in all its manifestations.

Whatever your gaze falls upon, tell yourself, 'I am giving this all the positive value it has for me'.

I expect you're feeling a more positive tone to today compared to yesterday – that's the idea anyway.

Set the lighting and temperature as required. Arrange blanket on the floor. Lie down on your back, knees bent, soles of your feet flat on the floor. Allow your lower back to broaden and sink into the floor. Keep breathing. Place your arms by your sides. Moving from the one point 6 cm below your navel, slowly raise your torso off the floor until you feel the muscles in your belly contract. Keep breathing.

By now this should be starting to feel quite familiar and even comforting to you. If not, let go and surrender more.

Relax all muscle groups not being actively used in the raising motion, especially the back of your neck.

You'd be surprised how often and how much you contract the back of your neck without realizing it in the face of any new information or situation you unconsciously fear you can't control.

Hold the posture.

Do this in the spirit of enjoyment, rather than in the spirit of fighting with your own body. The idea is to learn gradually to cooperate with yourself at the deepest level. Hence the idea of re-harnessing or re-yoking yourself.

Breathe slowly. Count 36 cycles of inhalation and exhalation. Scoop the loop.

As you inhale, feel the breath travel up the rear of your backbone to the top of your brain. As you exhale, feel the breath travel down the front of your backbone into your pelvic floor, thus forming a loop of chi. Eventually, you just find yourself doing this spontaneously all the time. That's when your spirit is dancing.

Lower your torso slowly till your entire back is lying flat again. Let your lower back sink into the floor. Lengthen your spine. Relax everything. Keep breathing. Count 3 cycles of inhalation and exhalation. Repeat the entire process of raising and lowering the torso 9 times. Place your palms on your belly. Mentally repeat the word 'strength' 9 times.

Turn onto your front. Stretch your legs out straight behind you, feet together. Place your palms on the floor, just to the outside of your shoulders. Lengthen your spine, especially the back of your neck. Keep breathing. Pull your buttocks and the muscles of your lower back inwards towards the spine. Moving from the one point below your navel, slowly raise your torso approximately 10 cm from the floor. Maintain the inward pull of the buttocks and lower back muscles. Relax all other muscle groups, especially at the back of the neck. Breathe more slowly. Count 9 cycles of inhalation and exhalation. Lower your torso slowly to the floor. Repeat the sequence 3 times through. Focusing awareness on your buttocks and lower back, mentally repeat the word 'strength' 9 times.

Are you feeling strong?

Roll to your right and lie on your back. Bend your legs at the knees. Place your soles flat on the floor, legs together. Stretch your arms out to the sides perpendicular to your torso to form a 'T'. Turn your head to face your right hand. Turning from the one point below your navel, let your legs slowly fall over to the left until your left knee is on the floor. Keep breathing. Feel the stretch across your torso. Breathe more slowly. Count 9 cycles of inhalation and exhalation.

Moving from the one point below your navel, slowly draw your legs straight and turn your head till gazing up at the ceiling. Turn your head to face your left hand. Turning from the one point below your navel, let your legs slowly fall over to the right until your right knee is on the floor. Keep breathing. Feel the stretch across your torso. Breathe more slowly. Count 9 cycles of inhalation and exhalation.

Moving from the one point below your navel, slowly draw your legs straight and turn your head till gazing up at the ceiling. Place both palms on your chest. Mentally repeat the word 'strength' 9 times. Roll to your left. Come onto all fours. Let your head hang down. Relax the back of your neck. Keep breathing. Moving from the one point, slowly stand up. Fold and stow the blanket. Be aware of how you're feeling in your body now.

Don't try and change it or do anything with it. Simply observe without prejudice.

11.17 am

Moving from the one point, walk slowly to the bathroom. Empty your bladder and bowels as required. Relax. Keep breathing. Wash. Say hello to yourself in the mirror. Wink conspiratorially.

Why not – you may as well have a laugh while you're doing this, or what's the point.

11.30 am

Moving from the one point, walk slowly to the kitchen. The only thought in your mind is, 'I am walking slowly to the kitchen'. Prepare breakfast. The only thought in your mind is, 'I am preparing breakfast'. Place palms approximately 10 cm above the food.

Think of all the energy involved in getting the food onto your plate. Think of all the people involved in the chain that made it possible. Think of the forces of nature required for the food to exist. Think of how painful it is to starve. Be thankful for the food you are about to eat. Let the essence of that gratitude, stream out through your palms into the food. Eat breakfast. Chew each mouthful 18 times.

Other than yesterday, has breakfast ever felt like this before? Did you ever feel as if you were communing with gods with each mouthful like this?

The only thought in your mind is, 'I am eating breakfast'.

Quite a late breakfast – more of a brunch in fact. But hell, it's Sunday, so go on, enjoy yourself. Bon appetit!

12.00 pm

Moving from the one point, walk slowly to the designated space. Take the pad and pen.

Here we go – it's work time again.

Sit in the chair. Relax. Keep breathing. Lengthen your spine. Broaden your hips and shoulders.

Don't skip these instructions just because they keep being repeated. They are repeated because they comprise the fundamental building blocks of a sound inner and outer personal structure.

Allowing one entire page for each, make a list of the following personal attributes, (placing one attribute as a header at the top of each page).

These are the essential components of invincibility itself, so pay full attention – this is a crucial moment in the training.

'Always-on willingness and readiness on your part to perceive, acknowledge and accept the paradox inherent in every aspect of existence and to appreciate its significance, especially when things appear to be moving against you.'

The traditional Taoist take on this is that every phenomenon has a yin aspect and a yang one – a bright side and a shadow. For everything visible about it, there is at least as much that's invisible. It's the every cloud has a silver lining approach – but also encompassing the fact that every silver lining has a cloud. Yin and yang move in a cycle, one transforming into the other and back again. To get hooked on only one half or the other is foolish, hence the old Taoist advice to greet all new information with 'not necessarily good, not necessarily bad'. It's all to do with lighting and camera angles – in other words, which way you look at something. So cease trying to draw conclusions or take positions. The way will reveal itself but only when you do away with preferences. Like this you are able to sit with the paradox inherent in every situation without your peace of mind being perturbed by the fluctuations in mood caused by the yin–yang cycle, at which point, the way, The Great Way, or Tao, rates you as being so sussed, it showers you with all the blessings you can handle.

'Always-on willingness and readiness to exercise the resilience to optimize conditions, as they present themselves – to always see and make the most of your external reality, especially in the face of disappointment and deflation.'

The requisite level of acquiescence implicit in being willing to sit with the paradox is not to suggest lying down and dying in the face of obstacles. You take every opportunity and do everything within your power to ameliorate and optimize conditions as you find them, as and when you can, while remaining in warrior mode – centred and peaceful – and as and when you can't, you relax, accept how things are and get on with something else – something productive – until the knots in your situation undo themselves.

'Always-on willingness and readiness to relax your body and mind and to breathe freely and – where possible – slowly, especially in the midst of stressful situations.'

Whether in passive or active mode in relation to the yin–yang cycle of events, your effectiveness at dealing with the task at hand, whatever that might be, as you work, rest or play, is heightened immeasurably by having sufficient energy flowing through your system to keep you fuelled up. When you're physically tense, you become mentally tense and stop breathing properly – you hold your breath without even realizing it. Conversely, when you let your breathing flow freely and consciously relax your muscles, your mind will relax as well. Then you start thinking more clearly and see exactly how to proceed with maximum effect.

'Always-on willingness and readiness to access and activate the courage to continue contributing to the world around you and letting it contribute to you, especially when it or you feels irrelevant.'

The currency of the world of the world is not primarily money, it's contributing – money is just a symbol of the measure of your contribution, as in being willing to give of your time, focus and energy to the world around you. The more you give, the more you receive. But the giving must come first. Because half the time events are in the yin phase of the cycle, it will often appear you are just giving out and getting nothing back. This is merely on account of the time delay until the yang phase recommences and brings your ship back in for you. During these times, it often appears that the world of the world doesn't even want your contribution, that you are somehow irrelevant. This

131

often coincides with you feeling what's going on in the world is irrelevant to you. You are momentarily disconnected – or so it would appear at the time. To see yourself through such times – out in the cold – requires courage, the inner fire of the heart, to warm things up inside till the story swings back to the yang again.

'Always-on willingness and readiness to enter a state of full surrender to the pull of the mystery, especially when apparently stepping into the abyss.'

Your rational mind, your pride, your vanity may be telling you to go one way, while inside you the tug of the unknown is stronger. Don't ever resist it, even when it feels as if you're freefalling into the void without a parachute. The mystery will catch you and deliver you to safety. This means learning to follow rather than force.

'Always-on willingness and readiness to clear and focus your mind by repositioning your internal stance in relation to reality, especially during stressful phases of information and responsibility overload.'

Trusting that reality as you see it is just reality as you see it – a subjective truth rather than an actual one. You can totally alter what you perceive as external reality by shifting where you're observing from – changing the lighting and camera angles, in other words. But you have to be willing to do that rather than cling on to a view that's making you miserable, as we are so strangely won't to do.

'Always-on willingness and readiness to touch the world with love, by exercising humaneness, compassion, good humour, kindness, fairness, mercy and forgiveness in your dealings, both with others and with your own self, especially when confronted by prejudice, meanness and pettiness, either in others or yourself.'

It's just too easy to slip back and default in varying degrees to self-interested, fear-induced ruthlessness, selfishness, ill-humour, unfairness, cruelty and resentment in relation to others, especially when confronted by it in others, or when trapped in a judgemental state yourself and it requires conscious willing to override that urge and go the love and generosity route at all times. It's the positive energetic flow this love provokes in the world of the world that protects you and brings you whatever you need in the moment.

'Always-on willingness and readiness to be humble enough to listen and quiet enough to hear the still small voice of the spirit within you and wise enough to do what it tells you, especially when it apparently runs counter to the strict demands of your rational mind.'

The voice of your guiding spirit, your innermost self, or the Tao – no one knows whence it comes – is always there talking to you. You probably had experience of that yesterday from time to time. If you follow it, your life takes on a new dimension. You start walking in the realm of the gods, while still firmly on the ground. But you have to let yourself be still enough within, to let the monkey-mind chatter subside enough to be able to hear what it's telling you. And that re-quires a certain degree of humility – to let go of self-importance and shut up long enough to listen.

133

'Always-on willingness and readiness to access and exercise tenacious strength and limitless stamina in order to follow through and complete, especially when faced with an apparently insurmountable obstacle.'

It's not easy getting started doing something new, no matter the challenge facing you. There is always resistance from that deluded part of you which wants and expects things to remain the same forever. But once you've got started, the really hard bit is maintaining the drive to follow through to completion. For this you need tenacity and stamina. Tenacity and stamina are primordial qualities and are not restricted to the privileged few. You access them, simply by choosing to access them. It's all done with the mind.

'Always-on willingness and readiness to retreat to the fallback position of knowing you are nothing but pure energy, vibrating at the appropriate set of frequencies to hold you in shape, informed by pure consciousness and animated by pure love. In the ultimate sense, you, as you've come to know yourself, do not exist at all, especially when your very existence is threatened.'

So if, heaven forbid, it all disappeared tomorrow – your relationships, your home, your work, your fun, your body even, at least you'd still be doing OK as an amorphous bundle of pure energy, consciousness and love. In the greater scheme of things, everything after that is really pure bonus. And what a lovely bonus it is. Rejoice for whatever you have right now.

134

'Always-on willingness and readiness to be honest and sincere in all your dealings with others and yourself, especially when confronted by dishonesty and insincerity in others or yourself.'

Without this the world – your world – gets very messy. We all trip up every now and then and tell the odd fib, occasionally even a full-blown outright lie. And that's OK as long as you realize that every time you do it, the world lies to you in return. Or, at least, you find yourself lying to yourself, which eventually ties you in knots. By observing yourself at such times, noting the lie but not punishing yourself for it – simply acknowledging it – combined with the willingness to be honest and, hence, sincere in all your dealings, over time you'll find yourself being honest pretty much all the time, both with others and yourself. This doesn't necessarily mean revealing your hand at all times. Discretion must also be part of the equation. Being sincere about what you say and do, doing what you say you will – or at least telling those involved if you've changed your mind – rather than just messing them about, is what makes the world of the world's engine turn. The more lies you throw into the machine, the more convoluted the results. The more honesty you throw in, the smoother it all runs for you. It's not to do with morals. It's plain common sense.

'Always-on willingness and readiness to dedicate your life to serving the greater flow of energy expressed in humankind at large, especially when tempted by the glitter of personal gain or glory.'

It's always tempting to focus on what you can get out of a situation in terms of personal gain, as opposed to what you can put in. However, once followed this path only leads to self-limitation, emptiness, lack of fulfilment and general misery, however much money or status you have. To be in the flow of the Tao, The Great Way, you must approach every situation and every person with the question on your lips, 'How can I best serve here?' Seeing your life in terms of how you can serve as opposed to how you can be served, gives it meaning and purpose beyond the shallow materialism normally associated with success. This doesn't mean you must close yourself off to receiving, as if receiving is bad and giving is good. It's your divine duty to open yourself to receive as well as give, it's just that your focus remains on serving rather than being served.

'Always-on willingness and readiness to cease attempting to draw conclusions, especially when apparently being forced to make a decision or take a position.'

Rarely will you be granted a moment of wide-screen panoramic vision huge enough to afford you the perspective to see the whole picture of your existence and how it sits against the background pattern of the greater reality. Trying to draw conclusions beyond the most basic physical facts – fire burns, ice freezes and you need air to breathe, water to drink, food to eat, shelter to house you and company to warm your heart – merely gets in the way of you following the Tao where it's trying to lead you. Everything is just as it is for this moment. In the very next moment from now, everything in your entire universe could radically change. Flexibility of mind is what's required, to remain open to all possibilities all the time and thus not place limitations on how grand reality can actually be for you and others.

'Always-on willingness and readiness to let go of your version of how reality is or should be, especially when it appears your survival depends on you defining your reality.'

The insecure part of you that fears death and clings to life and therefore wants everything to remain the same forever, attempts to fool you into vainly attempting to make reality as you see and know it, into a solid shape, box it, label it and store it away. This is the best way to kill life and miss the actual show. Remain open to reality as you know it being predicated merely on the set of opinions you're holding on to at the time and set it free to dance how it wants to around you. When you give reign to reality to do that, it dances much more prettily.

Flip back through the pages and carefully read each of the above 3 times, focusing on the meaning as it occurs to you (as opposed to trancing out).
Not so you buy it, not so you agree – as always, listen but decide for yourself – just that you entertain the concepts lavishly enough to get the fullness of them to impact on your mind. Your mind will automatically reject any detail or idea it doesn't need. Just read and let the sense wash over you.

12.30 pm

Moving from the one point, slowly place the pad by your side. Stand up. Take stock of where you are and how you feel.

Perhaps a bit heady?

Stand facing north, feet together, arms by your sides, palms facing in. Slowly rotate your forearms to position your palms facing outwards. Bend your elbows slightly. Slowly raise your arms out to the sides to shoulder-level, as if holding up a 2 m long log across your chest.

The invisible log represents your new good. Hold it with grace, care and aplomb.

Keep breathing. Relax.

The following derives from a simple pa kua move and is to make you energetically more receptive to your new good, by walking you in a clockwise circle in a fully receptive posture, by trapping the positive attributes of the subtle centrifugal force in your energy field.

With your arms in log-carrying position, turn to your right. Moving from the one point, walk slowly in a clockwise circle just within the periphery of the designated space. Set your gaze looking into the centre of the circle you're describing on the floor. As your weight falls through your left foot, place awareness in your right hand. As your weight falls through your right foot, place awareness in your left hand.

This is to prevent your monkey mind from having too much space to chatter.

Sensitize yourself to the energy flowing between your two palms.

This automatically activates awareness of your entire energy field.

As your arms grow tired, relax your shoulders more. Keep breathing. Your only thought is, 'I am stepping into the new now'. Complete 36 circuits. Stop and stand, feet together, facing north. Slowly, moving from the one point, lower your arms to your sides and rotate your forearms until your palms face in. Say out loud, 'I am ready and willing to take on the new now'.

As you call it, so it shall be.

1.00 pm

Sit in the chair. Pick up the pad and pen. Turn to the page headed:

> *'Always-on willingness and readiness to perceive, acknowledge and accept the paradox inherent in every aspect of existence and to appreciate its significance, especially when things appear to be moving against you.'*

Beneath it, write:

> *'I am now willing and ready to perceive, acknowledge and accept the paradox inherent in every aspect of my existence and to appreciate its significance, especially when things appear to be moving against me.'*

Then write it again and again until you've filled the entire page with it. Do this without thinking. Just write. Repeat this process with each of the headings, writing the following affirmations respectively:

> *'I am now willing and ready to exercise the resilience to optimize conditions as they present themselves – to always see and make the most of my external reality, especially in the face of disappointment and deflation.'*

'I am now willing and ready to relax my body and mind and to breathe freely and, where possible, slowly, especially in the midst of stressful situations.'

'I am now willing and ready to access and activate the courage to continue contributing to the world around me and letting it contribute to me, especially when it or I feel irrelevant.'

'I am now willing and ready to enter a state of full surrender to the pull of the mystery, especially when apparently stepping into the abyss.'

'I am now willing and ready to clear and focus my mind by repositioning my internal stance in relation to reality, especially during stressful phases of information and responsibility overload.'

'I am now willing and ready to touch the world with love by exercising humaneness, compassion, humour, kindness, fairness, mercy and forgiveness in my dealings, both with others and with my own self, especially when confronted by prejudice, meanness and pettiness, either in others or myself.'

'I am now willing and ready to be humble enough to listen and quiet enough to hear the still small voice of the spirit within me and wise enough to do what it tells me, especially when it apparently runs counter to the strict demands of my rational mind.'

'I am now willing and ready to access and exercise tenacious strength and limitless stamina in order to follow through and complete, especially when faced with an apparently insurmountable obstacle.'

'I am now willing and ready to retreat to the fallback position of knowing I am nothing but pure energy, vibrating at the appropriate set of frequencies to hold me in shape, that in the ultimate sense, I, as I've come to know myself, do not exist at all – especially when my very existence is threatened.'

'I am now willing and ready to be sincere in all my dealings with others and myself, especially when confronted by dishonesty and insincerity in others or myself.'

'I am now willing and ready to dedicate my life to serving the greater flow of energy expressed in humankind at large, especially when tempted by the glitter of personal gain or glory.'

'I am now willing and ready to cease attempting to draw conclusions, especially when apparently being forced to make a decision or take a position.'

'I am now willing and ready to let go of my version of how reality is or should be, especially when it appears my survival depends on me defining my reality.'

There's something about writing down such thoughts repeatedly that makes them go in more directly than when speaking. Something about taking the thought out of the mind, where it remained hitherto invisible – making it visible as words on a page somewhere out here in the world of the world and then feeding that back into your brain through your eyes – that makes it more real for your mind and it only takes something to be real for your mind, for it to become real for you, as well you've learned by now. Don't be afraid of auto-brainwashing, however. Your mind will still reject information it doesn't require, however many times you repeat it in writing.

1.30 pm

Place the pad down by your side. Moving from your centre, stand and walk slowly to the bathroom. Empty your bladder and bowels as required. Wash. Look at your face in the mirror. Out loud, say, 'I love you'.

If you say it and mean it, you can be sure the trend will catch on and someone will soon be saying it to you too. And no nicer words are there to hear when delivered with sincerity.

Walk slowly to the designated space. Stand facing north, feet spread as wide apart as you can get them, knees lightly bent.

Feel, enjoy and surrender to the stretch. However, at the slightest hint of lower back pain or strain, or indeed leg-muscle spasm, stop at once and if necessary seek medical help. Meanwhile, stretching your adductor muscles and pelvis like this opens up a whole new store of hitherto damned up vitality, intimately connected and useful to your

143

sexual functions, so expect this to make you feel quite sexy within 10 minutes or so.

Drop slowly forward from the hips.

Remember, this isn't a competition. It's a meditation, so don't force or rush it and don't bounce.

Place your palms on the floor in front on you, shoulder-width apart, arms straight. Exhale fully. Inhale slowly, bend your arms and slowly bring your chest towards the floor, allowing your heels to come off the floor. Exhale and slowly straighten your arms, pushing your hips backwards until back in the original position.

This Taoist push-up, adopted from the fabled 'Red Dragon' series of forms, will strengthen your arms and shoulders most effectively, thus stabilizing your emotional state and increasing general brain-to-arm-to-hand coordination and dexterity, as well as making your upper body look way better – always a desirable thing, however much you may deny it. The move may be easy for you, in which case repeat it 18 times in all, otherwise follow the instructions as below.

Repeat twice more. Your only thought is, 'I'm doing this to grow stronger'.
It's helpful to remind yourself why you're doing it as it reduces the potentially dangerous tendency to fight with your body mid-move.

Moving from the centre, draw yourself slowly upright. Inhale. Exhale and jump your feet together. Stand with feet together, arms hanging at your sides. Take stock of where you are and how you feel.
You probably have a fair amount of energy rushing through your hips, genitals, chest, upper back, shoulders and arms. Take a moment to appreciate it.

Bend your knees lightly. Tuck your sacrum under to lengthen your spine from waist-level down. Drop your chin slightly to lengthen your spine from shoulder-level up.
This is a pa kua standing meditation intended to exponentially increase inner strength and unify it into a single force, capable of smashing walls. But don't try that at home – at least not without a good pickaxe and a couple of sturdy dustsheets.

Make fists. Nestle your left fist into your left hip joint. From the one point, turn a bit to the left and place your right fist on top of your left fist, to form a small cross. Using the intersection formed by your two wrists as a lining-up point, gaze down at the floor. Keep breathing. Allow stillness to flood you.
It will now if you let it. This posture is famous for its peace-inducing properties.

Your only thought is, 'I am still – I am strong'.

Simply drop without ceremony any other thoughts that pop into your mind that you find are not adding to your general peace and happiness. You are under no obligation to think anything in particular – or even at all if you can manage it.

Count to 180.

Mild challenge this. If you find yourself flagging, simply relax more and breathe more slowly, thinking, 'I am still – I am strong'.

Repeat on the other side, placing your left wrist on top of your right. Sit down. Take stock of where you are and how you feel.

Don't just let the moment and all its swirling sensations pass without noting it. This is your life, after all.

Pick up the pad. Read each page aloud, reciting every repetition of each affirmation as many times as it appears on the page. Emphasize different syllables in different words at random with each repetition.

This is just to stop you going in a trance. Stay awake.

Allow the meaning of each affirmation to impact on your psyche. Detach the lists. Stow the lists. Place the pad by your side. Moving from the one point, slowly stand.

2.00 pm

Set the alarm to go off at 2.33 pm. Spread the blanket. Place the book-as-pillow accordingly. Lie down, knees bent, soles flat on the floor, arms by your sides. Keep breathing. Relax your shoulders. Make loose fists. Place fists just over each side of the centre of your breastbone. Take stock of where you are and how you feel. Inhale deeply. Exhale, chanting the sound, 'HAAAAAAAH!' resonantly until all the air is emptied from your lungs.

This is the sound Taoists associate with healing the heart in order to boost your courage – courage to live and courage to love. If you let them, the vibrations of the upper harmonics created with your voice will resonate throughout your thoracic cavity like low-tech ultrasound, healing away all your fear, resentment and stuckness, to make way for love – of which the ability to give and receive freely in the appropriate way at all times is a crucial component of invincibility.

Repeat this 8 more times. Simultaneously pummel your chest gently but firmly. Keep your shoulders relaxed.

This has a similar effect of dislodging any remaining stuck heart chi and stimulating the flow of fresh chi to facilitate love to flow freely in your life.

At the end of the last of the 9 exhalations, stop pummelling suddenly. Sensitize yourself to the fizzing sensation in your chest.

This is the heart chi in a momentarily heightened state before it settles down and starts circulating through your system.

Open your fists and let your arms drop slowly to your sides. Place awareness in your palms.

Other than your face through mouth and eye movements, your palms are the two surfaces through which you conduct most of your intercourse with other people. The following is to train your palms into the giving or serving mode – that you may be served in turn (don't worry, your turn will come).

Keep breathing. On each inhalation, feel your life-force gathering around the one point below your navel. On each exhalation, feel your life-force travel in two separate streams up to your shoulders, down your arms and into your palms. Your only thought is, 'Love keeps me safe'.

Sensitize yourself to the feeling of fullness in your palms. This is chi ready to be given to the world via whomever or whatever you touch. Now you're familiar with it, you can induce it to happen with a simple out-breath, whenever required for healing purposes and even self-defence.

2.33 pm

Moving from the one point, slowly roll to your right and up onto all fours. Let your head hang down. Tuck your sacrum slightly under. Feel your spine elongate. Keep breathing. Your only thought is, 'I am breathing'.

It doesn't get much more basic or important than that.

Take stock of where you are and how you feel. Slowly stand, fold and stow the blanket and book, face north, feet at shoulder-width, arms hanging by your sides. Keep breathing. Bend your knees lightly. Tuck your sacrum slightly under. Tuck your chin slightly in. Elongate your spine from waist-level down and from shoulder-level up.

Turn your right foot out to a 45° angle. Moving from the one point, lean your full body weight on your right foot. Step your left foot directly forward, facing due north. Transfer your body weight fully onto your left foot. Moving from the one point, draw your body weight back onto your right foot and step your left foot back behind your right foot, placing it down, toes first facing out at a 45° angle (north-west). Transfer all your body weight onto your right foot.

This is a tai chi stepping back and forth move, designed to occur without strain through a simple pendulum-like motion initiated from the one point.

Moving from the one point, draw your body weight back onto your left foot again and step into the forward stance – then back, then forward and so on, until you feel the momentum of your one point moving back and forth in space is causing you to advance and retreat without effort. As you advance and retreat, let your arms swing naturally as a counterweight. Step forwards and backwards like this 180 times.

This requires entering a mild, childlike trance state and fully letting go into the experience. Simply by the repetition of this move you are training your spirit to step lightly into and out of situations, to advance and retreat, as it were, without ever losing your balance or inner poise, psycho-emotionally, practically or socially speaking.

Change sides with a hop (so now your right foot will be stepping to and fro) and repeat likewise 180 times. Your only thought is, 'I am advancing and retreating with balance, poise and grace'. Stand with feet parallel at shoulder-width, knees bent, sacrum tucked under, chin tucked in. Keep breathing. Allow your energy to sink and settle around the one point. Your only thought is, 'Here I stand strong'.

Because there you do stand strong – and nimble-footed too by now. It's important to acknowledge it. This moment will serve as an anchor in your memory, a metaphor for your unconscious mind to relate back to in times of need, during all subsequent engagement with the world of the world.

3.12 pm

Set the alarm for 4 pm. Spread the blanket and place the book-as-pillow. Lie down, knees up, soles flat, arms by your sides. Read carefully 3 times and memorize the following instructions from 'place the book down', up till, 'pick the book up'.

Place the book down. Close your eyes. Sink into the awareness of being just your bones. With that, incorporate awareness of being flesh. With that, incorporate awareness of being fluids. With that, incorporate awareness of being nerves. With that, incorporate awareness of being pure energy. With that, incorporate awareness of being pure consciousness. With that, incorporate awareness of being pure love. With that, incorporate awareness of being invincible. With that, incorporate awareness of simultaneously being human. Hold all this awareness simultaneously. Let it boost your self-esteem. Keep breathing.

Because you were so bravely willing to strip yourself right back to the bone and were OK enough with that to keep going, it's safe for you now, without too much risk of you losing your invincible perspective, to take on a few of life's little indulgences, such as flesh, body fluids and a nervous system, which, in the context of being a field of pure energy, consciousness and love, is bound to help boost your self-esteem a bit. This is naturally crucial to the process, as with self-esteem you feel worthy of life's gifts.

4.00 pm

Pick the book up. Take stock of where you are and how you feel. Stand slowly, facing north, feet together, arms hanging naturally by your sides. Draw your awareness back into the centre of your brain and witness the following from there. Keep breathing. With its epicentre in the one point below your navel, envision an egg-shaped, light-filled energy field surrounding and extending out from the physical parameters of your body by 2 m, above, below, behind, before and to the sides of you. See this field comprised of two fusing sub-fields, moving through each other, each spinning around you in opposite directions, clockwise and counterclockwise at the speed of light – 186,000 miles per second. Your only thought is, 'This energy is protecting me'.

> That's quite a feat, not just your ability to visualize it but also its ability to spin like that. Make that strong in your mind. It's crucial to your invincibility. With this force-field fully activated, no harm will come to you.

4.12 pm

Moving slowly from the one point, bow to the north, east, south and west respectively, turn off lighting as required and walk to the bathroom. Empty your bladder and bowels as required. Wash.

> Feel the release, the change of mood, the drop in intensity.

Change into outdoor clothes and footwear. Walk slowly to the kitchen. Drink water. Take stock of where you are and how you feel. Check the time. Tell your unconscious mind to keep track of the time and return you home by 5.30 pm.

> Your unconscious mind works perfectly as a clock all the time, constantly counting the beats, making fine adjustments for variations in the planet's tilt and even taking into account local time zones. It's just a simple matter of trusting it and being perceptive enough to listen when it tells you the time, or anything else for that matter.

Gather your keys, money, this book and mobile phone (to be kept in the off-position except for use in an emergency) and stow them on your person. Leave the building. Turn right. Walk approximately 3 km round the block in a clockwise direction.

> Clockwise, to reinforce the energetic flow of you rebuilding yourself.

If no block is available to walk round, go approximately 1.5 km and turn back. Whatever your gaze falls upon, tell yourself, 'I have imbued this with the beauty and light I see in it'.

> This is not to diminish the beauty itself. On the contrary, this is to re-inforce your awareness of how brilliantly magnificent you are to have channelled this primordial essence called beauty and gone and im-bued everyone and everything you see with it.

Whomever you pass, see or meet, think, 'I have imbued this person with the beauty and light I see in them'. Unthreateningly, humbly instigate polite eye contact with whomever you pass or meet.

> This is a basic gesture of acknowledgement and respect all too easily overlooked and with your protective force-field, as well as being

153

fundamentally empty of self, you have nothing to fear from any interaction that may result. Trust the field to screen out all negativity and only introduce positive, helpful people into your orbit from now on. If you must have a prayer in this respect, let it be, 'Protect me from all time-wasters', as that covers just about everything.

Open your mind to the possibility of striking up conversation with anyone you pass or encounter, including total strangers and make yourself energetically available to it should the opportunity arise. If the opportunity does arise to converse with a stranger or someone you know, place your right palm on your solar plexus (upper abdomen) while you talk, keep breathing and witness the proceedings from the centre of your brain.

Your solar plexus is where you receive the energetic imprint of the person you are dealing with, whether in the flesh, over the phone, by email, or even when just thinking about them. If their energy is vibrating at a level too low to resonate harmoniously with yours, thus producing a harmful effect on your field or person, you'll feel the pain of it right in the solar plexus. Keeping your hand here helps remind you to relax and keep your breath flowing, while protecting you from the energetic shock of any possible negative energy being transmitted by the other.

Should this situation arise, choose to see only the potentially positive qualities in the person or people you engage with.

Basically whichever primordial quality you choose to see in the other, is the quality that will grow. See the scoundrel and that's what you get. See the Buddha and that's what you'll get. They may still act like a scoundrel but they'll do it in a Buddha-like way so it won't hurt so much. Hence always remain fully awake when dealing with others, except for those you share a bed with, of course.

Whichever qualities you see in them, tell yourself, 'I have imbued this person with this quality I see in them'.

And then you have to marvel at the fantastic capacity others have of pulling off the act.

5.30 pm

Walk back in the building. Change back into the brighter indoor outfit. Walk to the bathroom. Empty your bladder and bowels as required. Wash. Say hello to yourself in the mirror – out loud.

And have a laugh – it's OK.

Walk to the designated space. Set the lighting as required. Stand facing north, feet together. Bow to the north, east, south and west.

But don't just pay lip-service to it. All parts of the process are as important as each other – or unimportant, depending on whether you choose to honour the proceedings of your life or not.

Walk to the kitchen. Prepare a snack – as energy rich as possible – and some tea.

And don't confuse energy with sugar.

Place snack and tea on a tray. Moving from the one point, carry the tray into the designated space. Sit carefully in the chair. Place the tray on your lap. Hold your hands approximately 10 cm above the food, palms down.

Be aware of all the people and energy involved along the chain, responsible for this food being on your plate. Feel gratitude. Let this gratitude be transmitted through your palms into the food. Eat the snack. Chew each mouthful 18 times. Your only thought is, 'I am chewing this food – I have imbued it with all the enjoyment it has for me'.

Drink the tea. Stand carefully. Take the tray back into the kitchen. Walk to the designated space. Sit on your heels. (If this is uncomfortable, sit in the chair and push your buttocks firmly into the seat.) Sensitize yourself to the sensation of your stomach processing the information contained in the food. Keep breathing. Place your right palm on your solar plexus (upper abdomen). Feel the warmth of your palm penetrate your stomach.

This to speed up and enhance the digestive process.

Envision the midday sun shining there, lighting up the whole of the inside of your body.

Hitching a ride on the digestive energy here a bit to light up your world. It's up for grabs so you might as well.

Envision this light extending to fill your entire egg-shaped energy field, above, below, before, behind and to the sides of you. Your only thought is, 'I am this light'.

6.00 pm

Take stock of where you are and how you feel.

Hopefully a fair bit lighter by now.

Moving from the one point, walk slowly to the bathroom. Empty your bladder and bowels as required. Wash and take care of the essentials. Pay yourself a compliment out loud, while looking in the bathroom mirror.

'You're looking good, kid' – that kind of thing but elaborate or otherwise at your discretion. You'd be surprised how much this helps your social confidence.

Change into your low-key social event outfit. Walk to the designated space. Take the mirror. Sit in the chair.

Just because you're all dressed up doesn't mean you can't humble yourself by sitting quietly in a chair. Observe how your adrenalin flows more strongly in Pavlovian reaction to getting dressed to go out. Don't do anything about it. Don't judge it good or bad. Simply observe and notice.

Keep breathing. Tuck in your chin slightly to elongate your spine from shoulder-level up. Tuck in your sacrum slightly to elongate your spine from waist-level down. Broaden across your shoulder and hip girdles. Soften your muscles, especially the back of your neck and your buttocks.

It has probably struck your attention by now, how quickly your shoulders and buttocks go into the contracted mode without your having realized it.

Relax your shoulders, elbows and wrists and hold the mirror so you can gaze into your own eyes. Read carefully 3 times and memorize the following instructions from, 'Draw your consciousness back into the centre of your brain', up to, 'Sharpen your gaze and bring your reflection back into focus'.

Draw your consciousness back into the centre of your brain and gaze at the reflection of your eyes from there. Allow your features to dissolve until you disappear. Your only thought is, 'I am pure energy'. Expand your scope of vision to take in your entire energy field. Your only thought is, 'Pure energy is invincible'. Place awareness in the one point below your navel. Keep breathing. Concentrate your consciousness in the centre of your brain. Your only thought is, 'I am pure consciousness'. Expand your consciousness to fill your entire egg-shaped energy field. Your only thought is, 'Pure consciousness is invincible'. Keep breathing. Sharpen your gaze and bring your reflection back into focus. Place the mirror down.

This disappearing and reappearing trick is to strengthen metaphysical resilience and flexibility. This process should have given you a strong enough hit of experiencing yourself as pure consciousness, which if you relaxed through it, should have you feeling rather exhilarated by now.

6.23 pm

Moving from the one point, stand up. Stand facing north with feet shoulder-width apart, arms hanging by your sides. Bend your knees slightly. Tuck in your chin slightly to elongate your spine from shoulder-level up. Tuck in your sacrum slightly to elongate your spine from waist-level down. Broaden across your shoulder and hip girdles. Soften your muscles. Keep breathing. Breathe more slowly.

For the duration of 9 slow inhalation–exhalation cycles, gently shake your fingertips as if shaking off water. Transfer all your body-weight onto your left foot. Raise your right foot a few cm off the ground. For the duration of 3 slow inhalation–exhalation cycles, shake the toes of your right foot as if shaking off water. Place your right foot down. Shift your entire body-weight onto your right foot. Raise your left foot a few cm off the ground. For the duration of 3 slow inhalation–exhalation cycles, shake the toes of your left foot as if shaking off water. Place your left foot down.

> This shaking-off process is to divest you of any pride you may have felt just now in having achieved a moment of pure consciousness. Because as soon as you congratulate yourself – as you inevitably will in some form – pure consciousness evaporates. Shaking that off keeps your energy circuits clear. You'll also find the physical sensation of energy in your palms quite enlivening as you do the next process. There are many doctors in China who have full faith that such regular shaking prevents cancer, because of how it encourages you to divest yourself of stagnant chi, which otherwise leads to disease.

Transfer your body-weight until it's falling 50 per cent through each foot. Bend your elbows slightly. Raise both arms straight out in front, palms out, as if pushing against a wall. Keep breathing. Maintain the posture for the duration of 9 slow inhalation–exhalation cycles. With each inhalation, envision energy gathering around the one point, forming a compressed ball of light.

Both the ball and the light are metaphorical, not literal, and are used as a device to focus your mind to activate your energy. The energy is not metaphorical, it's real as steel.

With each exhalation, envision releasing enough energy from the ball of light around the one point, to travel up in two streams, one to each shoulder, then down along the outside of each arm, into the centre of each palm and out into infinity beyond in two straight lines of infinite length.

This is a classic chi kung move, used to train your chi to transmit into infinity. Say, for instance, you have a project for which you need a large dose of follow-through to complete. You project your chi through the image of the work to be done into infinity beyond, and the forward thrust of that will carry you through to completion. Or say you wish to repel the energy of someone whose energy you feel would be harmful to you, physically or psychically, from a distance. You direct your chi through them into infinity beyond and the forward thrust of that will then be ample to do the trick.

You can use it for healing too – whether together or far apart from your 'patient'. Direct your chi through them, preferably sending it directly through the affected part and into infinity beyond. The forward thrust of that will push the diseased energy out of them. But it doesn't even have to be used consciously. Simply by doing the process, you set off your energy almost automatically in such a way that your consciousness is able to penetrate any situation and move through it into infinity beyond, thus increasing the possibilities for what you will to be done. The fact that the energy has to pass through your chest on its way out, thus infusing it with heart, ensures that you use it wisely and compassionately, not selfishly, ruthlessly or dangerously simply for your own gain.

Lower your arms slowly. Straighten your legs.

7.03 pm

Sit on your heels. (If this is difficult, sit in the chair and push your buttocks back into the seat). Take stock of where you are and how you feel.

You may be feeling excited so allow your energy levels to normalize and settle.

Make fists. Relax your shoulders, elbows and wrists. Keep breathing. Place your fists in front of your chest. Pummel your chest gently. Simultaneously, chant the sound 'HAAAAAAAH!' continuously and with the most possible resonance. Continue for the duration of 9 slow inhalation–exhalation cycles. Towards the end of the last cycle, stop pummelling suddenly. Sensitize yourself to the fizzing sensation in your chest. Allow it to spread throughout your body. Your only thought is, 'I am pure love'. Keep breathing. Allow it to spread beyond your physical parameters and fill your entire egg-shaped energy field. Your only thought is, 'pure love is invincible'.

Just in case you start getting carried away on the power, you bring your heart centre into the equation. This process is repeated here, not for a dearth of processes to choose from but because repetition is the **161** best way of instilling information and this process is an important piece of information. Not only does it activate your heart fire and thus, by extension, your courage and ability to give and receive love freely, rather than closing down and living in fear, all mean and psycho-emotionally shrivelled as a result, but it also stimulates your thymus gland, intimately connected to your immune system (a fairly crucial aspect of invincibility, you must agree), through its production of T-cells.

It also stimulates the flow of energy and blood throughout your cardio-vascular and respiratory systems, thus helping ensure the emperor – your heart – keeps on ticking away for as long as humanly possible. And because of all of that, doing it tends to make you feel happy and bold within 10 minutes or so. It's important, in other words and to cut a long story short, so it is repeated to make more of an impact on you and thus be potentially influential in getting you to do it on some kind of regular basis, post-training. But that, along with many other tips for continuing the effect post-training, will be dealt with at the end of the training, as you'd expect. I mention the post-training phase at this stage of the proceedings purposely to start introducing the idea that life certainly goes on after this and the training will go with you, if you want it to – or by now, pretty much even if you don't want it to. But back to the plot.

7.23 pm

Moving from the one point, stand, facing north, feet together, arms by your sides. Rotate your forearms back till your palms face in. Relax your elbows. Slowly swing both arms forward and raise to chest-level. Make a fist in your right hand. Place your left palm over your right fist to shield it. Bow to the north. Turn and bow to the east. Turn and bow to the south. Turn and bow to the west. Turn off lights as required. Gather your keys, money, this book, and a mobile phone in case of emergency. Go somewhere unfamiliar in the vicinity or within a short drive, where you'll be required to talk to and interact, to some extent, with others in a social environment, where there'll be a bit of noise and colour for approximately 1 hour.

> This isn't just a mindless repeat of last night's escapade. For a start your whole mind-frame is diametrically opposite. Rather than starting out from a place of utter emptiness, you are starting out from a place of utter fullness – full of energy, consciousness and love. This is the celebration of your nascent invincibility.

There is no need to look at any clocks, wristwatches or other timepieces. Let your unconscious mind keep track of the time for you. The chosen venue could be a bar, pub or club, preferably not the same venue as yesterday evening – somewhere you never or rarely frequent and wouldn't normally think of frequenting. As you walk in, tell yourself, you are nothing but pure love in action. Keep repeating this to yourself: 'I am nothing but pure love in action'. Let your gaze fall discreetly on each of the people present, one by one. Take your time. Take stock of where you are and how you feel. Lengthen the back of your neck and from the waist down. Broaden across your upper back and shoulders. Soften your chest. Allow your warmth to flow. Observe yourself from the centre of your brain. Observe your surroundings likewise. Keep breathing. Move from the one point.

As your gaze falls on each person, tell yourself, they are nothing but pure love in action. Engage in whatever commerce is required in observing appropriate protocol. As before, if this requires buying a drink, it is recommended to keep it alcohol free. If that could cause you undue stress, keep it to one glass of something light.

Introduce yourself to at least one person you don't know, preferably the one you'd be most scared to normally and not the one you spoke to yesterday evening – unless they're the only one there, in which case, good luck, it should be an interesting bit of dialogue. As you approach them, remind yourself, they are nothing but pure love in action. Assure them warmly you're not an oddball or cult-member. Explain you're doing personal development training and are required to talk to someone you don't know, whom you'd normally be too afraid to approach. Show them the book. Point to this instruction. Have a laugh together. Notice one quality in them you'd like to acknowledge. Acknowledge it. As you do, place a palm on their upper arm, with a subtly downwardly directed pull and make eye contact.

If, after this, the conversation goes no further, of its own accord, take your leave warmly and politely, move on to engaging the second most scary person for you and start again. Watch yourself doing it all from the centre of your brain. Relax. Keep breathing.

> There'll be a certain element here of losing your pride or vanity – the potential to make a proper Charlie of yourself, in fact. However, only by throwing yourself into the unknown like this, can truly quantum personal growth surges occur. In any case, if you relax and detach, while keeping your heart warm, it should be a lot of fun.

164   Keep repeating to yourself: 'I am nothing but pure love in action'.

9.00 pm

Go home.

9.23 pm

Change into your bright indoor outfit. Walk to the bathroom. Empty your bladder and bowels as required. Wash. Say hello aloud to yourself in the bathroom mirror. Walk to the designated space. Set lighting and heating as required. Moving from the one point, stand, facing north, feet together, arms by your sides. Rotate your forearms back till your palms face in. Relax your elbows. Slowly swing both arms forward and raise to chest-level. Make a fist in your right hand. Place your left palm over your right fist to shield it. Bow to the north. Turn and bow to the east. Turn and bow to the south. Turn and bow to the west. Walk to the kitchen.

Prepare a very light, easily digestible meal. Place meal on a tray. Moving from the one point, carry the tray into the designated space. Sit carefully in the chair. Place the tray on your lap. Hold your hands approximately 10 cm above the food, palms down. Be aware of all the people and energy involved along the chain, responsible for this food being on your plate. Feel gratitude. Let this gratitude be transmitted through your palms into the food. Eat the food. Chew each mouthful 18 times. Your only thought is, 'I am chewing this food – I have imbued it with all the enjoyment it has for me'. Stand carefully. Take the tray back into the kitchen. Walk to the designated space.

Part of the value of repetition is to teach you not to go to sleep on something just because it's familiar, not to be blind to the beauty and magnificence around you just because you've seen it a thousand times before. Stay awake.

10.23 pm

Sit in the chair. Sensitize yourself to the digestive process occurring in your gastro-intestinal tract. Take stock of where you are and how you feel. Reread aloud the contract you wrote out, signed and stowed.

> 'I, [your name here], do hereby solemnly swear to take myself through this training from start to end in one go, following the instructions precisely to the letter. I accept there will be difficult moments and passages and yet am willing to persevere regardless.'

This isn't done in order to punish yourself for possibly falling short. It is merely to provide an opportunity for you to observe yourself keeping an agreement with yourself, to whatever extent you've done that, and to watch how that makes you feel, without prejudice or seeking to draw conclusions about yourself.

While the immediate effects of the training are, as you see, profoundly impactful on the way you feel right now, the real, long-lasting effects unravel themselves subsequent to the actual training, in the days, weeks, months and even years that follow. Hence there's no need to try and draw conclusions about yourself and your integrity levels at this point. You're still a work in progress – by a long way as yet – as are we all.

10.30 pm

Keep breathing.

There's still much to be accomplished in the world.

Relax your muscles. Tuck your sacrum under to lengthen your spine from waist-level down. Drop your chin slightly to lengthen your spine from shoulder-level up. Touch all four fingertips of your right hand to the tip of your right thumb to form a bird's beak shape.

This one's powerful. There's a whole art based around the bird's beak and the ability to issue energy through it with force for martial purposes. Joining the fingertips to the thumb, opens up all 6 energy channels in the arm at once, thus facilitating an increase in velocity of the energy streaming through. The following exercise causes an energetic reaction that stimulates your power of concentration and opens up psychic vision, both of which are fairly essential to being invincible.

Relax your shoulders, elbows and wrists. Touch all four fingertips of your right hand to the tip of your right thumb to form the bird's beak. Relax your shoulders, elbows and wrists. Slowly raise your right hand until the apex formed by fingertips and the tip of your thumb is in line with your gaze. **167**

Gaze at the apex. Sensitize yourself to the stream of subtle energy flowing through your eyes between the apex and the centre of your brain. Keep breathing.

10.40 pm

Lower your right hand. Touch all four fingertips of your left hand to the tip of your left thumb to form the bird's beak. Relax your shoulders, elbows and wrists. Slowly raise your left hand until the apex formed by fingertips and the tip of your thumb is in line with your gaze. Gaze at the apex. Sensitize yourself to the stream of subtle energy flowing through your eyes between the apex and the centre of your brain. Keep breathing. Take stock of where you are and how you feel.

If you're feeling a preponderance of energy in your forehead, relax your face and let the energy sink down to the one point. The effects of the preceding on your ability to focus your mind are no doubt already discernable.

168

10.50 pm

Lower your left hand. Place your hands in your lap, palms up, back of the left hand resting in the right palm.

This is using your enhanced focusing power to serve.

Visualize the planet. Visualize all the people. Keep breathing. Feel your consciousness expand. Feel your consciousness expand until it's larger than your body. Feel your consciousness expand until it feels as if you're looking at the world from 1 m above the crown of your head. See the same happen to the consciousness of everyone on the planet. See your consciousness meet the consciousness of everyone on the planet. See your consciousness and the consciousness of everyone combined, form a sea of consciousness enveloping the planet a few metres above the ground all around. Visualize an opening in the centre of your chest. Feel as if you're breathing in and out through this opening.

This should be easy to feel after all that pummelling and chanting you've been doing (you hippie).

Feel a stream of love radiate from your chest and penetrate the sea of consciousness. Keep breathing until you see the entire sea of consciousness enveloping the planet completely suffused with love. Visualize openings in the centre of the sole of each foot.

This is to ground you, lest you're left with a preponderance of energy in your chest.

Feel as if you're breathing in and out through these openings. Feel streams of love radiate through the soles of your feet into the centre of the earth until the entire planet is filled with love. Keep breathing.

Without realizing it, when you get excited you tend to hold your breath. This causes excitement to turn into anxiety and is generally bad for your health.

Relax your shoulders, elbows and wrists. Raise your arms straight out in front of you, palms facing out, to shoulder height as if pushing against a wall. Visualize openings in the centre of the palm of each hand. Feel as if you're breathing in and out through these openings. Feel streams of love radiate through your palms until you feel fully connected to all that is, in this love. Lower your arms.

Are you feeling exhilarated?

Relax and detach. Keep breathing. Take stock of where you are and how you feel.

Don't do anything to shift it. Simply observe yourself without prejudice and carry on breathing.

11.15 pm

Moving from the one point, stand, facing north, feet together, arms by your sides. Rotate your forearms back till your palms face in. Relax your elbows. Slowly swing both arms forward and raise to chest-level. Make a fist in your right hand. Place your left palm over your right fist to shield it. Bow to the north. Turn and bow to the east. Turn and bow to the south. Turn and bow to the west.

> Say thank you to the Tao, even though it doesn't care. It serves to put you in a state of gratitude and that's important because that triggers grace, the milieu in which quantum leaps or so-called miracles take place.

Turn out the lights. Moving from the one point, walk to the kitchen. Drink water and prepare any bedtime drinks or snacks. Take any bedtime drinks or snacks to your sleeping place. Walk to the bathroom. Undress. Empty your bladder and bowels as required. Wash and take care of the essentials. Say goodnight and well done to yourself in the bathroom mirror.

> You have to admit you've done pretty well getting this far and have shown immense courage, fortitude – and shown yourself to be a good sport. The effects of all this are rather potent, wouldn't you say?

Put on nightwear if you wear any.

11.30 pm

Walk to your sleeping place. Set the alarm to go off at your usual Monday morning wake-up time. Get into bed. Lie back against the pillows, facing up. Keep breathing. Decelerate your breathing. Tell yourself, 'I now sleep deeply through the night, remain consciously in command as I dream, fly if I want, and awake 6 full minutes before the alarm rings, feeling refreshed, rejuvenated, revitalized and ready for something entirely new'.

The reason for programming yourself to beat the alarm by 6 minutes is merely to instil more confidence in the power of your mind. The 6 is purely arbitrary – 5 is too predictable and 7 too long.

Read the following instructions 3 times carefully from 'place the book down' up to 'pick up the book and open it', and memorize. Mark your place in the book.

Place the book down. Turn off the light. Close your eyes. Take stock of where you are and how you feel.

Do you like it? So far so good?

Sink your consciousness back into the centre of your brain, as if you had a third eye in the centre of your forehead, gaze out through it at the darkened room. Just before falling fully asleep, turn onto your right side. At some point during your dreams, examine your hands, front and back.

This will be most likely be a remarkable moment. As soon as you see your hands clearly – and the clarity is generally quite startling – you'll be able to take full command of the dream. From then on you can fly if you want to. But be careful not to go too high, unless fully experienced in dream-flying, in case you get blown away by solar winds. At the same time, if you can also scoop the loop, feeling the chi rise up the rear of your backbone on inhalation and dropping back down the front on exhalation, you'll have a dream so mind-buggering in its unifying effect on your unconscious and conscious mind, you'll probably be raving on about it for weeks afterwards. It may not happen immediately. It may take a few nights practising this style of falling asleep subsequent to the training for the conscious dreaming to kick in properly, but it will happen if you persevere. And I strongly recommend you do, as it tends to expand your consciousness exponentially.

4 monday (or last day of training)

reconstructed: the reintegration process

This is the transition process – going from retreat mode into the world of the world – it's the bit that seals all the work you've done. Remember to keep breathing slowly through it all, to remain mindful, even remain mindful of yourself forgetting to be mindful. Watch it all unfolding in all its convoluted glory, from the centre of your brain. Remember to keep your spine as long as possible and your shoulders and hips as broad as can be. Keep your chest soft and let your natural warmth flow freely. Relax all your muscles and sink your chi down to collect around the one point. Remember you have invested everyone and everything you see with all the value you perceive in them and you can invest them with any values you like from here on in. The world is up for grabs. Take it.

Wake up 6 minutes before the alarm. Take stock of where you are and how you feel.

Don't pass judgement on it. Don't try and change it. Simply notice it, breathe with it and let it be.

Spend a moment contemplating your dream if you can remember it. Pick the book up and open it. Tell yourself, 'I choose to enjoy this day come what may', 6 times. Lightly place the tip of the forefinger of each hand at the outer corners of your eyes on each side. Stroke ever so softly and slowly along the edge of the bone immediately under each eye until your fingertips are touching the top of your nose on each side by the inner corner of each eye. Stroke softly and slowly along the edge of the bone immediately above each eye until your fingertips are once again at the outside corner of each eye. Repeat this cycle slowly, softly and patiently 18 times. The only thought in your mind is counting the cycles. Keep breathing.

It pays to regulate your breathing pattern before you start the day in earnest, as it sets up a mental rhythm that will sustain you till you next fall asleep.

Moving your body from the one point 6 cm below your navel, walk slowly to the bathroom. The only thought in your mind is, 'I'm walking slowly to the bathroom'. Empty your bladder and bowels as required.

It would be impractical and nigh on impossible to give detailed instructions to cover you till you get to work or the equivalent, as you can imagine. So till 10 am you're on your own, so to speak. But I have every faith in you, as I hope by now you have in yourself, that you'll handle it all with utter aplomb.

From now till 10 am, do what you would normally on a Monday morning. Take this book, the contract and all the lists you've written with you wherever you go. Observe yourself from the centre of the brain. Keep breathing. Your only thought is, 'I am doing what I normally do'.

This should give rise to a whole flurry of commentary from your monkey mind. Thank it sincerely for its contribution. Observe it all from the centre of your brain without seeking to draw any conclusions.

175

10.00 am

This, of course, is assuming some kind of conventional work routine for the sake of keeping the training as universally applicable as possible – and imagining at my end that the greatest number of people reading this will be at some sort of place of work, probably surrounded by or in the company of others, getting on with whatever you get on with of a Monday morning. I realize this is probably quite a clichéd way of treating you, so if you are in a totally different situation to that – perhaps working at home alone, perhaps not working at all – then improvise.

Wherever you are, whomever you're with, whatever you're doing, take stock of where you are and what you feel like.

The influx of sensory and mental data might feel slightly overwhelming. Don't try and change that. Just relax, detach, observe and notice without prejudice. It doesn't matter.

Keep breathing. Relax your muscles. Tuck your sacrum under to lengthen your spine from waist-level down. Drop your chin slightly to lengthen your spine from shoulder-level up. Observe yourself from the centre of your brain. Soften your chest. Place awareness in the one point.

The idea is that this basic internal stance becomes, or is by now, second nature. However, you'll probably find you need to remind yourself to do it regularly and frequently even then.

Wherever you are, whomever you're with, whatever else you're doing, repeat this thought continuously so it becomes a repeated motif on the wallpaper of your mind: 'I am nothing but pure energy. Pure energy is invincible'. Look around you. Tell yourself, 'I have given this all the value it has for me'.

This whole illusion of the workplace, assuming that's where you are – and if you're not, I'm sure you have your equivalent – no longer need exercise its tyrannical hold over you. It is, at its most basic, nothing but pure energy, just like you and anyone present. As such it is no more solid or set in stone than a picture painted in water, when viewed from a sufficiently widescreen perspective.

And it's being able to maintain this perspective, while simultaneously maintaining the local view required to function effectively as a human being on the planet right now, even and especially if that involves dealing with a crisis, disaster or extreme situation of some kind.

You'll notice that it's perfectly possible – preferable even – effectively to take care of the task at hand on the one level, while on a deeper level, maintaining the fully meditative state that facilitates such perspective. This extends even to those times when much of your mind is in tatters with you going nuts about one thing or another. The deeper meditative state must prevail regardless and this will prevent you losing it altogether or at all.

This is important to remember because from here on in, or more precisely from noon, The Invincibility Training, in the greater sense, continues for the rest of your life, one way or another. There's no real turning back now. And the number one rule is to maintain the meditative state at all times, no matter what. That's what has you walking in the realm of the gods, with your feet firmly on the ground. And that when you fall out of it, as you inevitably will from time to time, you don't judge yourself harshly or punish yourself for it, you simply relax, detach, observe and notice, keep breathing and drop back in at once.

Whomever your gaze encounters, tell yourself, 'Whether they know it or not, this person is nothing but pure energy. Pure energy is invincible.' Whomever you chance upon, make eye contact and hold and touch lightly yet firmly on the upper arm for the length of one inhalation and exhalation, while saying hello.

This will come naturally if you let it. Don't contrive it. Don't fake it. Relax your shoulder, your arm, your hand and breathe. Transmit love and warmth, reassurance and comfort. It's what everyone wants – all the time. People just have funny ways of asking for it, that's all. And that's precisely what makes this game of hide and seek we play with each other and with ourselves – this daring masked ball, this crazy charade – so damn fun, exciting and riveting. So don't for a moment be afraid to show affection to another – in the appropriate way, of course – if done with confidence it will instantaneously cut through all the layers of artifice, but pretty much only for about the length of time your palm is making contact with their arm or shoulder. It's a brief parting of the veils through which two souls can meet. No need to labour the point. If you're working or hanging out alone, you may have to improvise using sonic touch over the phone or by email – or even just telepathically. The point of the process is simply to get you sharing the energy.

Otherwise carry on as normal.

Normal here obviously being used in the poetic sense, as there truly is no such thing in real life.

10.37 am

Wherever you are, whomever you're with, whatever you're doing, take stock of where you are and what you feel like.

You could be anywhere by now, with anyone, doing anything – I'm not to know, but wherever you are, whatever you're doing, whomever you're with, the crucial factor is maintaining the meditative space. I repeat myself purposely because repetition is the only way to make the information stay fully in circulation. After noon, I'll be handing the repetitions over to you to take care of and you'll be in charge.

Keep breathing. Relax your muscles. Tuck your sacrum under to lengthen your spine from waist-level down. Drop your chin slightly to lengthen your spine from shoulder-level up. Observe yourself from the centre of your brain. Soften your chest. Place awareness in the one point. Wherever you are, whomever you're with, whatever else you're doing, repeat this thought continuously so it becomes a repeated motif on the wallpaper of your mind: 'I am nothing but pure consciousness. Pure consciousness is invincible'.

This is not in any way to negate the previous assertion that you are nothing but pure energy. I should have mentioned this the first time it was introduced in the training but didn't wish at that point to break the meditative flow we had going there. What happens, if you haven't already felt it, is that you see clearly that energy, consciousness and love are merely three aspects of the same force or presence, call it the Tao, call it what you like – it's ineffable anyway. And as soon as you see your identity in that – nothing but pure energy, pure consciousness, pure love, nothing in fact but the Tao itself – you are fully invincible as there is nothing other than the Tao. So what would there be to overcome you? Nothing. You are invincible – or for the sake of officially completing the training – soon will be.

Whomever your gaze encounters, tell yourself, 'Whether they know it or not, this person is nothing but pure consciousness. Pure consciousness is invincible.'

The only way to remain invincible around others is to elevate them to the same realm as you when you deal with them, as opposed to dropping out of your realm into theirs – unless they're vibrating at an even higher frequency than you, in which case they'll pull you up automatically. You do this by seeing them as comprised of the same elements as you – pure energy, pure consciousness, pure love, call it what you will, the Tao – and honouring them in that state, while simultaneously honouring the disguise they even wear even unto fooling themselves.

Even in the midst of work-a-day reality, your mind is able to be fully in universal awareness and not even other people can pull you out of it, while simultaneously engaged with the level of thought required to get on with the task at hand, whatever that might be.

Choose one person – anyone will do – and verbally acknowledge them for one fine quality you see in them.

You'd think it would matter who you interact with but it's whoever the Tao first blows you towards with enough force to make you want to do it. It really doesn't matter what you think. Your own prejudices only limit what can happen between you anyway. This is about getting transpersonal – beyond the personal, with everyone you encounter – at least on the bedrock level beneath the masquerade.

If necessary, because of stilted delivery on your part, or through the unusual nature of what you're saying within the context, show them this instruction in the book.

I don't know and it would be wrong to assume anything – you probably have such well-developed social skills you don't need me telling you how to do it. However, you never know. You could be suffering a shyness attack. You may be feeling so deep inside from the training, you find you've totally forgotten how to do a basic thing like paying someone a compliment. So I'm merely covering as many bases as I can and hope your intelligence isn't feeling in any way insulted by it – that's quite the opposite of what I intend.

Allow whatever conversation this inspires to evolve naturally. Keep breathing. Observe yourself from the centre of your brain. Otherwise carry on as you normally would.

We're nearly at the end here and I don't know about you, but I'm starting to feel twinges of separation anxiety, as I generally do towards the end of a really fine piece of communing, for that's what we've been doing here you and I, one way or another.

But I have to let you go. I know that. And you have to let me go. We all have to let everything go one day. Hence the need for the training in the first place – so that through all the slings and arrows and in the face of all those storms, we stand strong and unvanquished. Nice speech – but it's not over till the fat Taoist sings.

11.07 am

Wherever you are, whomever you're with, whatever you're doing, take stock of where you are and what you feel like.

This even if you're in exactly the same place as you were at 10.00 am and 10.37 am, looking at the same view with the same people or alone. It's always new. This moment with everything as it is in the entire universe – and it's all interconnected – has never been before. This is all part of your ability constantly to let the past go and welcome the new instead. The light is constantly changing. Your angle too. Your body is undergoing different chemical processes every millisecond. It's all new. Honouring that lends you the power of the moment, wherein lies sanity – and nowhere else.

Keep breathing. Relax your muscles. Tuck your sacrum under to lengthen your spine from waist-level down. Drop your chin slightly to lengthen your spine from shoulder-level up. Observe yourself from the centre of your brain. Soften your chest.

Come on – let that love flow now.

Place awareness in the one point.

Let all sense of self sink into your lower abdomen.

Wherever you are, whomever you're with, whatever else you're doing, repeat this thought continuously so it becomes a repeated motif on the wallpaper of your mind: 'I am nothing but pure love in action. Pure love in action is invincible'.

Of all the three, this tan tien is by far the warmest. You can feel the qualitative difference. It's like immersing yourself in a warm bath of exotically fragrant oils, as opposed to straightforward warm water with maybe a drop or two of lavender. It's this warmth that conducts miracles or quantum events most freely – certainly more freely than in the cold – but that's obvious.

Whomever your gaze encounters, tell yourself, 'Whether they know it or not, this person is nothing but pure love in action. Pure love in action is invincible.'
And really see them shine from within. Be generous.

Choose one person – anyone will do – and do something notably generous and kind for them.
In a way this would be even better done with someone you have hitherto actively disliked or been prejudiced towards. This is about bursting through the illusory veil that separates us all from each other, with a gift of your spirit.

Do not expect or wait for thanks. Instead, inside, say, 'Thanks for this chance to serve.'
Truly if you think about it, while it's nice when someone thanks you for something you've done for them, it's nice but it's not the be all and end all of life itself – it's not as good as a cool glass of spring water on a sweltering day, for instance. That kind of relief from existential torment only arises from being in service mode – through giving with purity of self in the moment.

The thanks are not the reward. Even the blessings you'll receive from life in return are not the reward. The reward is having a moment of pure consciousness, love and energy in the flow of the Tao – because that you can't beat. It's no big deal anyway. We're only talking about

183

doing something generous for someone. It's not as if someone just asked you to dismember yourself out on the street or anything.

Otherwise carry on as you normally would.
I'd imagine your sense of normality would be growing pretty blurred by now.

11.37 am

Wherever you are, whomever you're with, whatever you're doing, take stock of where you are and what you feel like.
Even if it's still just you on your own sitting there waiting for something to happen – yes, it looks like you, it feels like you, it even smells like you – as well you know by now, all that is just a habit, a set of opinions about reality and who you were in relation to it, which you were previously clinging to but have now all but discarded, other than for occasional ceremonial use. Now, who you are, just like the world around you, is all up for grabs and you're going to grab it.

Keep breathing. Relax your muscles.
I can't stress how much I mean this – it's vital if you really want your energy to flow and give you this invincibility you want, that you relax your muscles. Not even for invincibility but just for common-or-garden old-fashioned simple peace of mind. Relax your muscles and your mind follows. Same the other way round of course, but it's a lot easier to focus on a muscle and get it to relax than it is to focus on

something as nebulous as your mind and get that to relax. That's a sure way to get even more stressed. But do it through your body, using your mind, as in mentally releasing the back of your neck right now even as we speak, for instance, and everything settles nicely into place again before you can say Jack Robinson – but not, as you already know, for long. No, that monkey mind of yours is not about to turn over and play dead. It will grab any opportunity to hijack your thoughts, so you have to remain vigilant. After a while it gets easier. But enough of all that.

Tuck your sacrum under to lengthen your spine from waist-level down. Drop your chin slightly to lengthen your spine from shoulder-level up. Observe yourself from the centre of your brain. Soften your chest. Place awareness in the one point. Wherever you are, whomever you're with, whatever else you're doing, repeat this thought continuously so it becomes a repeated motif on the wallpaper of your mind: 'I am invincible'.

That's it. The nub of the whole thing. You are invincible if you believe you are. And you'll believe you are if you tell yourself you are. Reality, as you know it, is up for grabs. It's either your monkey mind or you. Which is it going to be? You really didn't have to do this training at all. That's the joke of it all. But you knew that all along. When I say you didn't need it, I mean the you you've rediscovered by doing the training, which it turned out was there all along – just obscured by the moves your monkey mind was making all over the picture. So maybe you did have to do it after all. In any case, assuming you got this far in the book, you probably did it to some degree already anyway, so there's no point analysing whether you should have or not.

And yes, I admit I'm playing with you now. Not playing with your mind, of course – I mean playing with you as if we were two kids messing about at the back of the class at school. And it's fun. You may have

185

noticed it took a while for me to wind up the energy here enough to show myself in all my radiant ebullience. In fact, I merely held back, if indeed you think I did and attempted to confine my comments strictly to the text, out of respect, only gradually making my presence felt more as things progressed, once I felt I'd given you the chance to settle into the groove. But once I felt you starting to relax and get comfortable with the language and rhythm, not to mention the overall concept, I just couldn't resist poking my head out a bit more. And now, here we are just before saying bye bye, I really can't hold back anymore. It's been fun though, hasn't it? I'm sighing with contentment myself.

Whomever your gaze encounters, tell yourself, 'Whether they know it or not, this person is invincible'.

You are seeing straight to the spirit of the person now. To walk in the realm of the gods you have to elevate anyone in your company to that status with you. It's not an exclusive club.

Reread the contract. Dispose of the contract and all the lists you've written.

The contract was there merely as a metaphor for all the contracts you make with yourself and others – mostly implicit and unspoken or un-written – and was intended to demonstrate to you how you are with agreements. No judgement, good or bad, is relevant. It's merely a matter of relaxing, detaching, watching and observing. Any Buddha will tell you that.

Tell yourself you've just done something fantastic. Say out loud, 'I've just done something fantastic'. If anyone you happen to be around asks what, simply show them the book.

I'm joking but I mean it – show them the book.

Though that aside, even if you just managed to follow the book through to this point without doing the training per se – your mind has been visualizing you doing it all as you read, which is almost as good, almost as effective. You've done a great thing. You've allowed yourself to follow a meditative stream of mindfulness through a 64-hour sequence, whether in real time or not and have thus to all intents and purposes, if you follow the tenets of the I Ching, gone through a birth, death and rebirth process at the deepest level of your being, all the way from hexagram number 1 – The Creative, through to 64 – After Completion – which is pretty much where you'll be in a very short time from now – all ready to start fresh with the mystery as it takes you from here.

But before we part, it would only be right to discuss what happens from here and what you might expect, reaction, results and continuity-wise. What happens from here is that life will test you. It will test your mettle on every possible front – emotionally, psychologically, socially, professionally, financially, ethically and spiritually. And the deeper you went in the training, the stronger the tests will be. You'll have the opportunity within the following weeks and months to experience and deal with anxiety, panic, anguish, anger, over-excitability, jealousy, insecurity, low self-esteem, confusion, doubt and pretty much every other negative state you can think of, as the deeper layer of psychic toxins from way back slowly work themselves out of your system, as it would have been impossible, short of letting off a depth charge in your gut, to have expelled all those years of debris in one 64-hour time span. Not only that but whenever you have the courage to challenge radically the established order of your life, the established order of your life will challenge you. It's only fair. But behind it all is the Tao and, being the generative force of existence itself, the Tao is intrinsically benevolent and the tests it allows life to throw at you will be essentially hollow and insubstantial though it

187

may not appear that way when they occur. You will meet every test and you will come through winning. And you know why? Because you're invincible.

But just because I say so and just because you've just spent, as far as I know, 64 hours of your life proving your own invincibility to your-self, doesn't mean it will be handed to you on a plate. Naturally, you'll be required, should you wish to preserve and develop your invincibility, to practise regularly some or all of the processes from the training on some kind of regular basis, for only by constant repetition is Monkey ever really tamed for real. It's an ongoing process. To make it simple, here's a brief list of processes from the training, not necessarily in order of importance – each, any or all will suffice in abbreviated form to give you the juice you need to go on.

- Breathe freely. (Stop holding your breath).

- Lengthen your spine.

- Broaden your hips and shoulders.

- Soften your muscles.

- Sink your chi down to the one point.

- Make all your moves, no matter what they are, from the one point.

- Be mindful of what you're doing, saying, thinking and feeling at all times.

You are always doing one thing at a time even when it may appear otherwise.

- Relax, detach, observe and notice absolutely everything both in your mind and externally, from the centre of your brain.

- Let your love flow as warmth from your chest at all times.

- Scoop the loop.

- Do the Taoist sit-up.

- Do the Taoist cobra.

- Do the Taoist twist stretch.

- Do the Taoist hamstring stretch.

- Stand in the 'metal' Hsing I posture.

- Stand in the wall-pushing posture and channel chi through your palms.

- Bounce in the standing posture.

- Roll up into the foetal position.

- Walk counter-clockwise circles to dispel the past.

- Walk clockwise circles to step into the new.

- Stand in the T-shape posture, palms down to dispel negativity.

- Stand in the wide-open embrace posture to welcome your new good.

- Keep your observatory thoughts simple – for example, 'I am walking slowly to the kitchen'.

- Use affirmations throughout the day.

- Use affirmations before falling asleep.

189

- Fall asleep looking out through the centre of your forehead.

- Choose the kind of day you want when you wake up.

- Do the eye-socket massage.

- Do the ear-pressing technique.

- Make lists as described in the training.

- Approach anyone you want to even if they look scary.

- Spend time in silence.

- Remind yourself you are nothing but pure energy, consciousness and love and as such you are invincible.

- Be kind and generous to others without thought of personal gain.

- Be thankful for your food, liquids and just about everything else.

- Chew each mouthful 18 times.

- Remind yourself you have invested everything and anything you can think of with all the value it has for you and with all the qualities you see in it.

- Remind yourself that essentially when you break it all down, you, as you know yourself, do not actually exist.

- Remind yourself that essentially, when you break it all down, the world of the world as you know it, does not actually exist.

- Cease seeking to draw conclusions.

- Appreciate everything.

But, of course, you'll be tested. What would be the fun otherwise? You can't expect to experiment with reality like this without the inevitable slap-back being real also – or at least giving that appearance. (Always remind yourself that nothing is how it seems in the world of the world.)

But what you'll also find is that you withstand those tests with aplomb and that nothing, however painful, will actually get to you or radically rock you at the deepest level of your being again. Nothing ever could even before you did the training. It's just that now you know it.

You'll also find you have a heightened awareness of everything that's going on around you – not just in your immediate vicinity but any-where and everywhere you focus your attention or need to know about, however far away. Your psychic powers will be heightened. Your relationship with spirit, the Tao, your higher self – or however you wish to label that ineffable realm whence springs all your per-sonal power – will deepen exponentially. Your ability to guide things into your life you need will increase tenfold. Your happiness levels will increase exponentially. Your ability to recover almost instantly from bouts of any form of negativity will increase exponentially. Your relationships with others will become more honest and reward-ing. Your confidence and self-esteem will increase profoundly. Your stress levels will fall and your immune system will grow markedly stronger. Your entire life will move to a new level altogether and you'll find yourself walking in the realm of the gods but with your feet firmly on the ground.

You'll still be capable of being a total fool of course – you're only hu-man after all – but you will no longer beat yourself up over it and will, indeed, grow to love yourself, those around you and life in general, more and more with every passing breath. And if that's not enough for you, you want some pleasing.

191

12.00 pm

Congratulations. You have completed the training. You may now consider yourself invincible.

the instructions

as a stand-alone section

1

friday (or first day of training)

deconstruction: the undoing process begins

8.00 pm

(The next 24 hours are conducted in total silence. If you've been talking, stop now.)

- Take stock of where you are and how you feel.
- Insert earplugs.
- Stand with feet together in the centre of the designated space facing approximately due north.
- Place palms together in 'prayer position'.
- Bow discreetly acknowledging the four directions, turning slowly to each in turn, starting with east.
- Facing approximately due south, kneel down on the floor, knees together, sit back on your heels, and bending at the hips, allow your chest down onto your thighs. (Alternatively, if you find sitting on your heels impossible or unduly uncomfortable, sit firmly into the chair and lean forwards from the hips likewise).
- Place your hands behind you resting on your sacral bone at the base of your spine.
- Feel the stretch across your lower back.
- Visualize your kidneys filling with blood and energy.
- Count 9 cycles of slow inhalation and exhalation.
- Raise your chest away from your hips and sit straight.
- Using your mind, elongate your spinal column, feeling it lengthen from the

sacral bone at the base, through the back of the neck and into the upper brainstem within your skull.

- Using your mind, broaden your pelvic girdle, feeling your hips relax and spread – likewise your shoulder girdle, allowing your shoulders to slump.
- Feel all the energy racing round your brain and chest. Allow it to sink downwards and settle below the navel, imagining your pelvic girdle forming a bowl in which to receive it.
- Using your mind, scan all areas of your body for unnecessary muscular tension, starting at the crown of your head and working carefully down to the soles of your feet. Wherever you notice tension, let it go on an out-breath.
- Placing your palms down on the floor either side of your knees to balance yourself, stand up slowly, starting at your hips and slowly straightening your torso to the vertical position, your head coming up last.
- Keep breathing.

8.07 am

- Walk slowly to the bathroom.
- As the weight of your body falls onto your left foot, place awareness in your right hand. As the weight of your body falls onto your right foot, place awareness in your left hand.
- The only thought in your mind other than that, is, 'I am walking to the bathroom'.
- Remove clothing.
- Remove earplugs.
- Turn on the shower to hot. If no shower is available, run a hot bath.
- Empty your bladder and bowels as required.
- Place the book appropriately so as to keep it dry.
- Check the time on the clock.

8.12 am

- Take a 6-minute shower or bath.
- Wash your body in a brisk, yet gentle, loving manner, from the head down.
- As you do, say to yourself 6 times, 'I am not only washing the dirt off my body, I am cleansing myself of everything I've been clinging to consciously or unconsciously from the past, that no longer fully promotes my well-being.'

8.18 am

- Dry off carefully.
- Apply skin, hair and fragrance products at your discretion.
- Replace earplugs.
- Put your clothes on.

8.23 pm

- Walk slowly to the kitchen.
- As the weight falls on your left foot, place awareness in the right palm.
- As the weight falls on your right foot, place awareness in the left palm.
- The only thought in your mind is, 'I am walking to the kitchen'.
- Get the meal ready.
- Walk slowly to the designated space carrying the meal on a tray.
- As your weight falls on your left foot, place awareness in the right palm (holding the tray).

196

- As your weight falls on your right foot, place awareness in your left palm (holding the tray).
- The only thought in your mind is, 'I am walking to the designated space carrying a meal'.
- Sit comfortably on the chair.
- Place the tray on your lap.
- Hold your two hands over the meal, palms facing down, approximately 10 cm above the food.
- Be aware of the work of all the people involved along the chain of getting this food on your plate.
- Be aware of the intricate forces of nature responsible for its existence.
- Be aware of how painful it is to be starving.
- Be aware of the life-giving goodness in the food you are about to be filled with.
- Be thankful.
- In your mind, say 'Thanks'.
- Feel the subtle force of that gratitude exit through your palms and into the food.
- Mentally elongate your spine.
- Broaden your hips and shoulders.
- Relax your thoracic and abdominal cavities (chest and belly).
- Take a mouthful of food.
- Relax your jaw.
- Smile with your eyes.
- Chew the food in your mouth 18 times.
- Swallow the food.
- Repeat until the meal is finished.
- The only thought in your mind is, 'I am chewing this food'.
- Drink some fluid.
- As you do, the only thought in your mind is, 'I am drinking fluid'.
- Place both palms on your belly.
- Again, be aware of the work of all the people involved along the chain of getting this food on your plate.

- Be aware of the intricate forces of nature responsible for its existence.
- Be aware of how painful it is to be starving.
- Be aware of the life-giving goodness in the food you are about to be filled with.
- Be thankful.
- In your mind, say 'Thanks'.
- Feel the subtle force of that gratitude exit through your palms and into your belly.

9.06 pm

- Remove both hands slowly.
- Take hold of the tray.
- Stand up carefully holding the tray.
- Walk slowly to the kitchen.
- As your weight falls through your left foot, place awareness in your right hand.
- As your weight falls through your right foot, place awareness in your left hand.
- The only thought in your mind is, 'I am walking to the kitchen'.
- Place the tray down.
- Walk slowly to the designated space.
- As your weight falls through your left foot, place awareness in your right hand.
- As your weight falls through your right foot, place awareness in your left hand.
- Sit in the chair.
- Mentally elongate your spine.
- Broaden your hips and shoulders.
- Relax your thoracic and abdominal cavities (chest and belly).
- Mentally relax your stomach and intestines.
- Allow all your mental energy to settle and sink downwards into your stomach and intestines.
- Keep breathing.

9.15 pm

- Press your buttocks back into the seat of the chair.
- Relax your arms and let them hang by your sides.
- Lean forward from the hips until your hands are hanging by the sides of your shins just below knee-level.
- Make fists.
- Relax your shoulders, elbows and wrists.
- Pound a gentle, steady drum roll on the fleshiest part of the ridges of muscle, to the outside of the shins just below knee-level.
- Keep breathing.

9.19 pm

- Stop pounding.
- Raise your torso slowly to the upright position.
- Stand up slowly, head coming up last.
- Walk slowly to the kitchen.
- As your weight falls through your left foot, place awareness in your right hand.
- As your weight falls through your right foot, place awareness in your left hand.
- Take the remains of the meal from the tray.
- Wash the dishes or rinse and place them in a dishwasher.
- Relax your body, especially your shoulders and lower back.
- Keep breathing.
- The only thought in your mind is, 'I am washing the dishes'.
- Walk slowly to the bathroom.
- As your weight falls through your left foot, place awareness in your right hand.   **199**

- As your weight falls through your right foot, place awareness in your left hand.
- The only thought in your mind is, 'I am walking to the bathroom'.
- Empty your bladder and bowels as required.
- Wash your hands.
- Dry your hands.
- Rub oil or moisturizer into them.
- Walk slowly to the designated space.
- As your weight falls through your left foot, place awareness in your right hand.
- As your weight falls through your right foot, place awareness in your left hand.
- Your only thought is, 'I am walking to the designated space'.

9.45 pm

- Set alarm clock in designated space to go off at 10.00 pm.
- Spread the blanket on the floor.
- Place the approximately 8-cm thick book on the blanket in place of a pillow.
- Take a blindfold.
- Lie down on the blanket, face up, knees bent and soles of the feet flat on the floor.
- Read the following instructions, from, 'apply the blindfold', up to 'remove the blindfold', carefully 3 times through, picturing what it looks like and memorize.
- Apply the blindfold.
- Place your two palms on your lower abdomen below the navel so the fingertips of both hands meet, little finger tips, lightly touching the top of your pubic bone.
- Adjust your earplugs if necessary.
- Inhale fully.

- Start humming a continuous 'mmm' sound in a register comfortable for your voice, at moderate volume, until all the air is emptied from your lungs.
- Become aware of the vibrations this causes in the forehead and cheekbones.
- Repeat this inhalation and humming cycle twice more.
- Let your thoughts drift wherever they want to go (until alarm goes off).

10.00 pm

- Remove the blindfold.
- Stand up slowly, head coming up last.
- Relax your shoulders, elbows and wrists.
- Lightly place the tip of the forefinger of each hand at the outer corners of your eyes on each side.
- Stroke ever so softly and slowly along the edge of the bone immediately under each eye until your fingertips are touching the top of your nose on each side by the inner corner of each eye.
- Stroke softly and slowly along the edge of the bone immediately above each eye until your fingertips are once again at the outside corner of each eye.
- Repeat this cycle slowly, softly and patiently 18 times.
- The only thought in your mind is counting the cycles.
- Set the alarm to go off at 10.33 pm.
- Read the following instructions, from, 'apply blindfold', up to, 'remove the blindfold', carefully 3 times, picture what it looks like and memorize.
- Apply blindfold.
- Stand with feet at shoulder width.
- Bend your knees.
- Listen within to the rhythm of your heartbeat.
- Start swaying at the hips to the beat of your heart.
- Allow the movement to grow of itself.

- Let your arms go.
- Dance.
- Express yourself freely.
- Your only thought is, 'I'm dancing to the beat of my heart'.
- Remove the blindfold when the alarm goes off.

10.33 pm

- Walk slowly around the designated space in a counter-clockwise circle.
- As the weight falls through your left foot, place awareness in your right hand.
- As the weight falls through your right foot, place awareness in your left hand.
- Keep breathing.
- Simultaneously, concentrate your mind on a point, 6 cm below your navel.
- Walk, moving from this point.
- As you walk in counter-clockwise circles, tell yourself you are progressively stepping out of the past and leaving behind any energetic, psychic, intellectual, emotional, personal, professional and social ties that no longer serve your best interests.
- Keep one eye on the time.

10.49 pm

- Take the A4 pad and pen.
- Sit in the chair.
- Lengthen your spine.
- Broaden your hips.
- Broaden your shoulders.
- Relax your muscles.
- Keep breathing.
- Keep an eye on the clock.
- Write a list of everything that comprises your life, including your body, your possessions, your home, your relationships and your education.

11.01 pm

- Detach the pages or pages on which you've written.
- Hold them in your right hand.
- With your left hand, place the pad on the floor by your side.
- Stand up slowly.
- Hold the list up before you at chest height and tell yourself, 'The value I see and feel in all these aspects of my existence, is the value I have given them'.
- Stow the list.
- Stand facing approximately due north.
- Place your palms together in 'prayer' position.
- Bow gently from the waist.
- Bow to each of the other 3 directions, starting with east.
- Place your awareness in the point 6 cm below your navel.
- Initiating the movement from a point 6 cm below your navel, turn out all the lights and walk slowly to the bathroom.

203

- Until further notice, whatever your eye falls on, tell yourself, 'I have given this all the value it has for me'.
- Empty your bladder and bowels as required.
- Wash and do your essential bathroom routine.
- Adjust earplugs if necessary.

11.15 pm

- If a hot drink or snack is required, walk slowly to the kitchen and prepare it.
- Remember, until further notice, whatever your eye falls on, tell yourself, 'I have given this all the value it has for me'.
- When you've done that or if no hot drink or snack was required, initiating the movement from the point 6 cm below your navel, walk slowly to your sleeping place.
- Again, remember, until further notice, whatever your eye falls on, tell yourself, 'I have given this all the value it has for me'.
- Remove clothing.
- Put on nightwear if required.
- Set the alarm for 7.23 am.
- Get into bed.
- Lie back against the pillows, facing up.
- Keep breathing.
- Decelerate your breathing.
- Tell yourself, 'I now sleep deeply through the night and remain conscious as I dream and awake 6 full minutes before the alarm rings, feeling refreshed, rejuvenated, revitalized and ready for anything'.
- Read the following instructions 3 times carefully from, 'place the book down', up to, 'pick up the book and open it', and memorize.

- Place the book down.

- Turn off the light.
- Close your eyes.
- Take stock of where you are and how you feel.
- Sink your consciousness back into the centre of your brain.
- As if you had a third eye in the centre of your forehead, gaze out through it at the darkened room.
- Just before falling fully asleep, turn onto your right side.

2 saturday (or second day of training)

deconstruction: the undoing process deepens

7.17 am

- Wake up.
- Take stock of where you are and how you feel.
- Pick the book up and open it.
- Tell yourself, 'I choose to enjoy this day come what may', 6 times.
- Lightly place the tip of the forefinger of each hand at the outer corners of your eyes on each side.
- Stroke ever so softly and slowly along the edge of the bone immediately under each eye until your fingertips are touching the top of your nose on each side by the inner corner of each eye.
- Stroke softly and slowly along the edge of the bone immediately above each eye until your fingertips are once again at the outside corner of each eye.
- Repeat this cycle slowly, softly and patiently 18 times.
- The only thought in your mind is counting the cycles.
- Remove earplugs.
- Place your palms over your ears.
- Press in to muffle the sound of the room.
- Remove the palms a centimetre or so to let in the sound of the room.
- Press in again and so on 18 times.

7.30 am

- Rolling to one side or the other, slowly get out of bed.
- Pick up the book and open it.
- Moving your body from the one point 6 cm below your navel, walk slowly to the bathroom.
- The only thought in your mind is, 'I'm walking slowly to the bathroom'.
- Empty your bladder and bowels as required.
- Wash, shower and take care of all the essentials.
- Dry off and put on the duller of the two indoor lounging outfits.
- Put in fresh earplugs.
- Look around you.
- Remember, until further notice, whatever your eye falls on, tell yourself, 'I have given this all the value it has for me'.

7.59 am

- Moving from the one point 6 cm below your navel, walk slowly to the kitchen.
- The only thoughts in your mind are, 'I am walking slowly to the kitchen' and 'I have given this all the value it has for me', in respect of whatever your gaze falls upon.
- Make hot and cold beverages as required and drink.

8.15 am

- Set the alarm in the kitchen for 8.45 am.
- Do whatever you like till the alarm rings.
- Do not eat.
- Do not leave the house.
- Your only thought is, 'I am now doing whatever I like'.

8.45 am

- Walk into the designated space.
- Stand with feet together facing approximately due north.
- Place hands together in 'prayer' position.
- Bow to the north.
- Turn and bow to the east.
- Turn and bow to the south.
- Turn and bow to the west.
- Whatever your gaze falls upon, tell yourself, 'I have given this all the value it has for me'.
- Set the lighting and temperature as required.
- Arrange blanket on the floor.
- Lie down on your back, knees bent, soles of your feet flat on the floor.
- Allow your lower back to broaden and sink into the floor.
- Keep breathing.
- Place your arms by your sides.
- Moving from the one point 6 cm below your navel, slowly raise your torso off the floor until you feel the muscles in your belly contract.
- Keep breathing.

- Relax all muscle groups not being actively used in the raising motion, especially the back of your neck.
- Hold the posture.
- Breathe slowly.
- Count 18 cycles of inhalation and exhalation.
- Lower your torso slowly till your entire back is lying flat again.
- Let your lower back sink into the floor.
- Lengthen your spine.
- Relax everything.
- Keep breathing.
- Count 3 cycles of inhalation and exhalation.
- Repeat the entire process of raising and lowering the torso 9 times.
- Place your palms on your belly.
- Mentally repeat the word 'strength' 9 times.
- Turn onto your front.
- Stretch your legs out straight behind you, feet together.
- Place your palms on the floor, just to the outside of your shoulders.
- Lengthen your spine, especially the back of your neck.
- Keep breathing.
- Pull your buttocks and the muscles of your lower back inwards towards the spine.
- Moving from the one point below your navel, slowly raise your torso approximately 10 cm from the floor.
- Maintain the inward pull of the buttocks and lower back muscles.
- Relax all other muscle groups, especially at the back of the neck.
- Breathe more slowly.
- Count 9 cycles of inhalation and exhalation.
- Lower your torso slowly to the floor.
- Repeat the sequence 3 times through.
- Focusing awareness on your buttocks and lower back, mentally repeat the word 'strength' 9 times.
- Roll to your right and lie on your back.

- Bend your legs at the knees.
- Place your soles flat on the floor, legs together.
- Stretch your arms out to the sides perpendicular to your torso to form a 'T'.
- Turn your head to face your right hand.
- Turning from the one point below your navel, let your legs slowly fall over to the left until your left knee is on the floor.
- Keep breathing.
- Feel the stretch across your torso.
- Breathe more slowly.
- Count 9 cycles of inhalation and exhalation.
- Moving from the one point below your navel, slowly draw your legs straight and turn your head till gazing up at the ceiling.
- Turn your head to face your left hand.
- Turning from the one point below your navel, let your legs slowly fall over to the right until your right knee is on the floor.
- Keep breathing.
- Feel the stretch across your torso.
- Breathe more slowly.
- Count 9 cycles of inhalation and exhalation.
- Moving from the one point below your navel, slowly draw your legs straight and turn your head till gazing up at the ceiling.
- Place both palms on your chest.
- Mentally repeat the word 'strength' 9 times.
- Roll to your left.
- Come onto all fours.
- Let your head hang down.
- Relax the back of your neck.
- Keep breathing.
- Moving from the one point, slowly stand up.
- Fold and stow the blanket.

9.10 am

- Moving from the one point, walk slowly to the bathroom.
- Remove earplugs.
- Empty your bladder and bowels as required.
- Relax.
- Keep breathing.
- Wash.
- Put in a new pair of earplugs or cotton-wool equivalent.

9.30 am

- Moving from the one point, walk slowly to the kitchen.
- The only thought in your mind is, 'I am walking slowly to the kitchen'.
- Set the alarm to go off at 10.20 am.
- Prepare breakfast.
- The only thought in your mind is, 'I am preparing breakfast'.
- Place palms approximately 10 cm above the food.
- Think of all the energy involved in getting the food onto your plate.
- Think of all the people involved in the chain that made it possible.
- Think of the forces of nature required for the food to exist.
- Think of how painful it is to starve.
- Be thankful for the food you are about to eat.
- Let the essence of that gratitude, stream out through your palms into the food.
- Eat breakfast.
- Chew each mouthful 18 times.
- The only thought in your mind is, 'I am eating breakfast'.
- When you've finished eating, do whatever you like till the alarm goes off.
- The only thought in your mind is, 'I am doing whatever I like'.

211

10.20 am

- Moving from the one point, walk slowly to the designated space.
- Take the pad and pen.
- Sit in the chair.
- Relax.
- Keep breathing.
- Lengthen your spine.
- Broaden your hips and shoulders.
- Make a list of everything bad or wrong about yourself.
- Absolutely everything.
- Don't hold back.
- Keep breathing.
- When you finish, sit still.
- Your only thought is, 'I'm sitting still'.

10.40 am

- Read each entry on the list.
- After reading each entry, mentally say, 'I have given this all the negative value it has for me'.
- Stow the list.
- Make a list of everything good or right about yourself.
- Absolutely everything.
- Don't hold back.
- Keep breathing.
- When you finish, sit still.
- Your only thought is, 'I'm sitting still'.

10.58 am

- Read each entry on the list.
- After reading each entry, mentally say, 'I have given this all the positive value it has for me'.
- Stow the list.
- Slowly, moving from the one point, stand up.
- Slowly walk in a counter-clockwise circle around the designated space 6 times, arms by your sides, palms facing the floor, leaving space for a small apple in each armpit.
- As you walk, tell yourself you are stepping out of everything bad or wrong about yourself, as well as everything good or right.

11.15 am

- Sit in the chair.
- Push your buttocks back firmly into the seat.
- Hang your arms by your sides.
- Make fists.
- Moving from the one point, lean your torso forwards until your fists are hanging just below knee-level to the outsides of your shins.
- Rhythmically pound with your fists on the fleshiest part of the ridge of muscle running down the outside of each shin just below knee-level.

11.18 am

- Stop pounding.
- Moving from the one point, slowly raise your torso till upright.
- Place your palms on your belly.
- Feel your digestive organs working.
- Keep breathing.
- Lengthen your spine.
- Broaden your hips.
- Relax.
- Moving from the one point, stand up slowly.
- Place the book where you can read it standing hands-free.
- Stand with feet together, facing due north.
- Pivot your right foot on the heel 45° to the right to face approximately north-east.
- Step your left foot directly forward approximately 1 m, facing approximately due north.
- Bend both knees slightly.
- Place your body weight 60 per cent on the back leg, 40 per cent on the front leg.
- Tuck your sacral bone at the base of your spine, slightly under to lengthen your spine from your waist down.
- Elongate the back of your neck, allowing your chin to drop towards your chest a little, to lengthen your spine from shoulder-level up.
- Subtly bow that part of your spine between the two, back away from your front.
- Place your right hand, palm as if pressing down on a tabletop flush with your body at waist height, forefinger in line with your navel.
- Place your left hand, as if pressing with the outer edge of the palm on a wall in front of you, whose base is directly in line and flush with your toes, so your left forefinger is in line with your nose.
- Keep breathing.
- Gaze out gently past your left forefinger.
- Relax and soften every muscle group.

- Let your bones support you and form the shape of your posture but let all your muscles relax and soften, even the front of your thighs.
- Keep your left knee directly above your left heel.
- Keep your right knee over the toes of your right foot.
- Keep an eye on the clock.
- Settle in for a 9-minute stretch of standing there without moving.
- Relax your shoulders.
- Breathe more slowly.
- Place awareness in the one point below the navel.
- Your only thought is, 'I am standing here like this'.
- Keep breathing.
- As your left arm grows heavier relax your shoulders more.
- Sensitize yourself to the flow of energy between your left hand and right.
- Maintain awareness in the one point below your navel.
- Sensitize yourself to the energy field, originating in the one point, enveloping your entire body and extending approximately 1 m from the physical periphery all around you: above, below, behind, in front and to the sides.
- Keep breathing.
- As your left arm grows heavier, relax your shoulders more.
- As your thighs grow tired, relax your hips more.
- Remain sensitive to the flow of energy between your left hand and right.
- Maintain awareness in the one point below your navel.

11.27 am

- Keep an eye on the clock.
- Moving slowly and purposefully from the one point, transfer your body weight entirely on to your right foot.
- Draw your left foot back until your heels are together.

215

- Draw your left hand downwards into the table-pressing position, forefinger in line with your navel, matching the position of your right hand.
- Pivot your left foot 45° to the left to face approximately north-west.
- Step the right foot forward approximately 1 m, foot facing approximately due north.
- Raise your right hand and place it in the wall-pressing position, forefinger in line with your nose.
- Distribute your body-weight 60 per cent on the left foot, 40 per cent on the right.
- Settle in for another 9-minute stretch of standing there without moving.
- Relax your shoulders.
- Breathe more slowly.
- Place awareness in the one point below the navel.
- Your only thought is, 'I am standing here like this'.
- Keep breathing.
- As your right arm grows heavier, relax your shoulders more.
- Sensitize yourself to the flow of energy between your right hand and left.
- Maintain awareness in the one point below your navel.
- Resensitize yourself to the energy field, originating in the one point, enveloping your entire body and extending approximately 1 m from the physical periphery all around you: above, below, behind, in front and to the sides.
- Keep breathing.
- As your right arm grows heavier, relax your shoulders more.
- As your thighs grow tired, relax your hips more.
- Remain sensitive to the flow of energy between your right hand and left.
- Maintain awareness in the one point below your navel.

11.36 am

- Moving slowly from the one point, draw your right foot backwards until your heels are together.
- Step around behind and turn so you're facing south.
- Place your feet shoulder width apart, both feet facing due south.
- Bend your knees a little.
- Gently bounce up and down a centimetre or two either way at first, gradually letting go more into the movement until your entire body is bouncing up and down.
- Maintain awareness in the one point below your navel.
- Keep breathing.
- Keep bouncing.
- Your only thought is, 'I am bouncing up and down'.
- Keep an eye on the clock.

11.45 am

- Stop bouncing.
- Settle into the posture.
- Bend your knees.
- Tuck your pelvis under.
- Elongate your spine, from the waist down and from the shoulder-girdle up.
- Keep breathing.
- Place awareness in the one point below the navel.
- Straighten your legs.
- Remove earplugs.
- Place palms over ears.
- Press in to close off the sound.

- Release to open it up.
- Close and release alternately 18 times.
- Adapt to the increase in general volume of sound.
- Sit in the chair.
- Listen to everything.
- Hear every sound.
- Identify none of them.
- Allow sounds without labels or description through your ears into the centre of your brain.
- Keep breathing.
- Every sound you hear, tell yourself, 'I have given this all the value it has for me'.

12.00 pm

- Moving from the one point, walk slowly to the bathroom.
- As your bodyweight falls through your right foot, place awareness in your left hand.
- As your bodyweight falls through your left foot, place awareness in your right hand.
- The only thought in your mind is, 'I am walking to the bathroom'.
- Empty your bladder and bowels as required.
- Wash.
- Change into your outdoor clothes.
- Moving from the one point, walk slowly to the designated space.
- Take the pad and pen.
- Write the following note:
  Excuse me for not talking – I'm doing a 24-hour silent contemplation as part of a personal development training programme – speak to you next time I see you.

- Fold the note and stow it somewhere safe and easily accessible on your person.
- If you don't wear a watch, take the alarm clock from the designated space and stow it accessibly and safely somewhere on your person.
- Turn off lights as appropriate.
- Put on your outside footwear.
- Put your keys in your pocket.

12.15 pm

- Check the time.
- Leave the building.
- Walk into the street.
- Stand still with the street door behind you.
- Look around you.
- Keep breathing.
- Turn left from the front door.
- Moving from the one point, walk slowly round the block or equivalent in a counter-clockwise direction for 30 minutes. If there is no possibility of walking a complete loop in 30 minutes, walk for 15 minutes and turn back.
- Everything you see, tell yourself, 'I have given this all the value it has for me'. Otherwise, your only thought is, 'I am walking along the street'.
- Keep an eye on the time.
- Lengthen your spine.
- Broaden your hips and shoulders.
- Relax all your muscles.
- If you meet anyone you know, show them the note and smile, using facial expression and hand gestures if required but do not speak or make any vocal sound.

219

12.45 pm

- Walk back into your building.
- Remove footwear.
- Change into the indoor lounging outfit you've been wearing till now.
- If required, walk to the bathroom to empty your bladder and bowels and wash.
- Otherwise, walk directly to the designated space.
- Set lighting as required.
- If you took the alarm clock out walking, replace it.
- Walk to the kitchen.
- Prepare a light lunch.
- As you prepare lunch, the only thought in your mind is, 'I am preparing lunch'.

1.00 pm

- Place lunch on a tray.
- Moving from the one point, walk slowly to the designated space carrying the tray.
- Sit in the chair.
- Place the tray on your lap.
- Place palms approximately 10 cm above the food.
- Think of all the energy involved in getting the food onto your plate.
- Think of all the people involved in the chain that made it possible.
- Think of the forces of nature required for the food to exist.
- Think of how painful it is to starve.
- Be thankful for the food you are about to eat.
- Let the essence of that gratitude, stream out through your palms into the food.

- Eat lunch.
- Chew each mouthful 18 times.
- The only thought in your mind is, 'I am eating lunch'.

1.30 pm

- Stand slowly.
- Walk to the kitchen carrying the tray.
- Leave the tray in the kitchen.
- Walk back to the designated space.
- Take the pad and pen.
- Sit in the chair.
- Relax.
- Keep breathing.
- Elongate your spine.
- Broaden your hips and shoulders.
- Be aware of the digestive process.
- Make a list of all your fears.
- Don't hold back.
- List every single fear you have.

1.47 pm

- Detach the list from the pad.
- Place the pad and pen down by your side.
- Read the list.

- As you read each entry, tell yourself, 'I have given this fear all the negative value it has for me'.
- Stow the list.
- Let your arms hang by your side.
- Make fists.
- Moving from the one point, slowly lower your torso towards your knees until your fists are by the outside of your shins, just below knee-level.
- Relax your shoulders, elbows and wrists.
- Pound rhythmically on the fleshiest part of the ridges of muscle, which run down the outsides of your shins just below knee-level.
- Keep an eye on the time.

1.55 pm

- Stop pounding.
- Place your palms on your belly.
- Be aware of the digestive process.
- Stand up.
- Set the alarm for 2.45 pm.
- Spread the blanket.
- Place the 10-cm thick book on the blanket to be used instead of a pillow.
- Lie down on your back, knees bent, soles flat on the floor, arms by your side.
- Read the following instructions, from, 'apply a fresh blindfold', up till, 'remove the blindfold', 3 times carefully and memorize.
- Apply a fresh blindfold.
- Allow your lower back to sink into the floor.
- Elongate your spine.
- Keep breathing.
- Become aware of all the bones comprising your skeleton.

- Tell yourself, 'I have given these bones all the value they have for me'.
- Mentally, become nothing but your bones.
- Your only thought is, 'I am nothing but these bones'.
- Remain being nothing but your bones.

2.45 pm

- Remove the blindfold.
- Lightly place the tip of the forefinger of each hand at the outer corners of your eyes on each side.
- Stroke ever so softly and slowly along the edge of the bone immediately under each eye until your fingertips are touching the top of your nose on each side by the inner corner of each eye.
- Stroke softly and slowly along the edge of the bone immediately above each eye until your fingertips are once again at the outside corner of each eye.
- Repeat this cycle slowly, softly and patiently 18 times.
- The only thought in your mind is counting the cycles.
- Roll to your right, come up onto all fours and stand up slowly, head coming up last.
- Stand facing north, feet 10 cm apart, legs straight but not totally locked at the knees.
- Moving from the one point, slowly lower your torso from the hips, as if drawing your chest towards your thighs.
- Keep elongating your spine.
- Keep breathing.
- Relax.
- When you've reached the comfortable limit of flexibility in the movement, support your torso by holding your lower legs or feet.
- Do not bounce.

223

- Feel the stretch through your hamstrings.
- Surrender to the sensation.
- Remain in the stretch for 9 slow inhalation and exhalation cycles.
- Your only thought is, 'I am hanging forward'.
- Bend your knees.
- Moving from the one point, slowly raise your torso from the hips, until fully upright, your head coming up last.
- Walk to the kitchen.
- Drink water.
- Walk to the bathroom to empty your bladder and bowels as required.
- Walk to the designated space.

3.00 pm

- Take the pad and paper.
- Sit in the chair.
- Make a list of every single bad habit you have.
- When you've finished read through the list.
- After each entry, tell yourself, 'I have given this all the negative value it has for me'.
- Detach the list and stow it.
- Make a list of every single good habit you have.
- When you've finished the list, read through it and after each entry, tell yourself, 'I have given this all the positive value it has for me'.
- Detach the list and stow it.

3.20 pm

- Place the pen and pad on the floor by your side.
- Stand up.
- Put in a new pair of earplugs or cotton wool equivalent.
- Stand facing south with your feet shoulder width apart, both feet facing due south.
- Bend your legs a bit.
- Listen within to the beat of your heart.
- From the one point below the navel, start to sway your hips in time with the beat.
- Allow the movement to slowly spread throughout your body until every part is fully animated in dance.
- The only thought in your mind is, 'I am fully animated in dance'.
- Keep an eye on the clock.

3.30 pm

- Stop suddenly and freeze in whichever position you're in.
- Hold the position.
- Keep breathing.
- Count 3 slow cycles of inhalation and exhalation.
- Realign your posture till standing perfectly straight again.
- Set the alarm to go off at 4.10 pm.
- Spread the blanket.
- Place the book for use as a pillow.
- Lie down on the blanket with the book under your head, facing up, knees bent, soles flat on the floor, arms by your sides.
- Read the following instructions carefully 3 times and memorize from, 'close your eyes', till, 'open your eyes'.

225

- Close your eyes.
- Draw your consciousness back into the centre of your brain.
- Keep breathing.
- Let your thoughts drift.

4.10 pm

- Open your eyes.
- Lightly place the tip of the forefinger of each hand at the outer corners of your eyes on each side.
- Stroke ever so softly and slowly along the edge of the bone immediately under each eye until your fingertips are touching the top of your nose on each side by the inner corner of each eye.
- Stroke softly and slowly along the edge of the bone immediately above each eye until your fingertips are once again at the outside corner of each eye.
- Repeat this cycle slowly, softly and patiently 18 times.
- The only thought in your mind is counting the cycles.
- Roll to your left.
- Go onto all fours.
- Stand up slowly.
- Reset the alarm to go off at 4.30 pm.
- Take the mirror.
- Sit in the chair.
- Relax your shoulders.
- Keep breathing.
- Hold the mirror in front of you.
- Let your gaze fall on the reflection of your own eyes.
- Stare into your eyes.

- Allow your facial features to blur and distort.

- Keep staring into your own eyes.
- Allow your face to disappear.
- Keep breathing.
- Every time your facial features reform, stare into your eyes and allow them to dissolve and disappear again.
- Your only thought is, 'I have disappeared'.

4.30 pm

- Put the mirror down carefully.
- Moving from the one point, stand up.
- Walk slowly into the kitchen.
- Make a hot drink – jasmine tea, green tea or plain boiled water.
- Take the drink into the designated space.
- Sit down.
- Drink it slowly.
- Your only thought is, 'I am drinking this slowly'.
- Feel the effects of the warm fluid passing through your stomach and gastrointestinal tract.
- Stand up.
- Take the cup back into the kitchen.
- Wash the plates from lunchtime or rinse and place in dishwasher.
- As you do, your only thought is, 'I'm cleaning the crockery'.
- Walk to the bathroom.
- Remove earplugs.
- Empty your bladder and bowels as required.
- Wash.
- Massage your ears gently but thoroughly between fingers and thumbs until they grow hot.

227

- Reinsert earplugs.
- Walk to designated space.

4.50 pm

- Take the pen and pad.
- Sit in the chair.
- Relax.
- Keep breathing.
- Make a list of everything in your life you'd like to leave behind you now if only you could.
- Don't hold back.
- List every facet of your being that no longer serves you, every complex that still hangs you up, every fear pattern that prevents you being free, every situation that holds you back, every relationship that impedes your full expression of love, every obstacle to you reaching full potential in this life.
- Take your time.
- Keep an eye on the clock.

5.10 pm

- Read through the list.
- After each entry, tell yourself, 'I am willing to let this dissolve now'.
- Note any fear or resistance arising as a physical sensation of tightness in the chest, belly or back of the neck.

- Tell yourself, 'I have given this the negative value it has for me'.

- Breathe slowly.
- Relax your chest, belly and the back of your neck.
- Stow the list.
- Moving from the one point, stand up slowly.
- Stand, feet together, arms by your sides, palms facing touching outsides of thighs, facing approximately due north.
- Bend your knees slightly.
- Tuck your sacral bone at the base of your spine, under a bit, to elongate your spine from waist-level down.
- Drop your chin slightly and soften the back of your neck, to elongate your spine from shoulder-level up.
- Moving from the one point, slowly raise your arms sideways to shoulder-height, to form a 'T' shape with your palms facing the floor.
- Relax your neck.
- Relax your shoulders.
- Rotate your arms at the shoulder joints slightly till your palms are angled to face behind you.
- Keep breathing.
- Extend your shoulder-tips away from your spine.
- Extend your elbows away from your shoulders.
- Extend your wrists away from your elbows.
- Extend your knuckles away from your wrists.
- But do not lock your elbows, wrists or knuckles.
- Let your skeleton make the shape of the posture.
- Relax and soften all your muscles.
- As your arms grow tired, relax your shoulders more.
- Keep an eye on the clock.
- Keep breathing.
- Think of the contents of all the lists you've made during the past 20 hours and 47 minutes or so.
- Imagine all that content mixed together and transformed into gaseous form in your upper abdomen.

- With each successive exhalation, feel this gas rising progressively into your chest, across into your shoulders, down your arms and being expelled through the centre of each palm, thence to dissipate in the air behind you.
- Repeat this for the length of 6 cycles of inhalation and exhalation.
- Moving from the one point, slowly rotate your arms back the other way, till your palms are angled to face the floor again.
- Slowly lower your arms to your sides.
- Notice the sensation of increased circulation across your chest and upper back.
- Keep breathing.

5.35 pm

- Arrange blanket on the floor.
- Lie down on your back, knees bent, soles of your feet flat on the floor.
- Allow your lower back to broaden and sink into the floor.
- Keep breathing.
- Place your arms by your sides.
- Moving from the one point 6 cm below your navel, slowly raise your torso off the floor until you feel the muscles in your belly contract.
- Keep breathing.
- Relax all muscle groups not being actively used in the raising motion, especially the back of your neck.
- Hold the posture.
- Breathe slowly.
- Count 36 cycles of inhalation and exhalation.
- Lower your torso slowly till your entire back is lying flat again.
- Let your lower back sink into the floor.
- Lengthen your spine.

- Relax everything.
- Keep breathing.
- Count 3 cycles of inhalation and exhalation.
- Repeat the entire process of raising and lowering the torso 9 times.
- Place your palms on your belly.
- Mentally repeat the word 'strength' 9 times.
- Turn onto your front.
- Stretch your legs out straight behind you, feet together.
- Place your palms on the floor, just to the outside of your shoulders.
- Lengthen your spine, especially the back of your neck.
- Keep breathing.
- Pull your buttocks and the muscles of your lower back inwards towards the spine.
- Moving from the one point below your navel, slowly raise your torso approximately 10 cm from the floor.
- Maintain the inward pull of the buttocks and lower back muscles.
- Relax all other muscle groups, especially at the back of the neck.
- Breathe more slowly.
- Count 18 cycles of inhalation and exhalation.
- Lower your torso slowly to the floor.
- Repeat the sequence 3 times through.
- Focusing awareness on your buttocks and lower back, mentally repeat the word 'strength' 9 times.
- Roll to your right and lie on your back.
- Bend your legs at the knees.
- Place your soles flat on the floor, legs together.
- Stretch your arms out to the sides perpendicular to your torso to form a 'T'.
- Turn your head to face your right hand.
- Turning from the one point below your navel, let your legs slowly fall over to the left until your left knee is on the floor.
- Keep breathing.
- Feel the stretch across your torso.

- Breathe more slowly.
- Count 18 cycles of inhalation and exhalation.
- Moving from the one point below your navel, slowly draw your legs straight and turn your head till gazing up at the ceiling.
- Turn your head to face your left hand.
- Turning from the one point below your navel, let your legs slowly fall over to the right until your right knee is on the floor.
- Keep breathing.
- Feel the stretch across your torso.
- Breathe more slowly.
- Count 9 cycles of inhalation and exhalation.
- Moving from the one point below your navel, slowly draw your legs straight and turn your head till gazing up at the ceiling.
- Place both palms on your chest.
- Mentally repeat the word 'strength' 9 times.
- Roll to your left.
- Come onto all fours.
- Let your head hang down.
- Relax the back of your neck.
- Keep breathing.
- Keep an eye on the clock.
- Moving from the one point, slowly sit back on your heels.
- If this is impossible or extremely uncomfortable, sit in the chair and push your buttocks well back in the seat.
- Slowly lower your chest towards your knees.
- Place your palms flat on the floor out in front of you, in line with your shoulders.
- Use your arms to support you and let your chest slowly drop closer to your knees – all the way down if you can but don't force it.
- Do not bounce.
- Relax your hips.
- Broaden across your hips and lower back.
- Sensitize yourself to the energy flowing between your sacral bone at the base

of your spine and your upper brainstem at the top of your spine, inside your skull, just under the central brain region.

- Keep breathing.
- Draw your consciousness back into the centre of your brain, just above the top of your upper brainstem.
- Keep breathing.
- Watch this all happening from the centre of your brain.

6.25 pm

- Moving from the one point, push your buttocks back and down and slowly raise your torso till you're sitting straight, arms hanging by your sides.
- Keep watching yourself doing all this from the centre of your brain.
- Keep breathing.
- Maintain awareness in the one point below your navel.
- Place your palms on the floor in front of you and using them as support, slowly stand.
- Walk to the bathroom.
- Empty your bladder and bowels as required.
- Wash.
- Walk to the kitchen.
- Prepare a simple dinner, requiring only 28 minutes preparation time or less, which you can then leave for 35 minutes while you shower or bathe and which will then be ready to eat at 7.30 pm.
- Your only thought is, 'I am preparing dinner'.

6.55 pm

- Moving from the one point below your navel, walk slowly to the bathroom.
- Remove earplugs.
- Place palms over the ears.
- Open and close the ears by alternately pressing and releasing the palms 18 times.
- Empty your bladder and bowels as required.
- Take a shower or bath.
- Keep an eye on the clock.
- Wash your body from the head down.
- As you wash your body, tell yourself, 'I'm cleansing myself of everything on all the lists I've written, including even the good points'.
- Tell yourself, 'I'm cleansing myself of the past. I am ready to take on the new now'.

7.15 pm

- Get out of the shower or bath.
- Dry off.
- Attend to all the essential grooming moves necessary for a relatively social evening.
- Keep breathing.
- Relax.
- Watch yourself doing all this from the centre of your brain.
- Looking at your reflection in the mirror, tell yourself, 'I have given what I see here all the value it has for me'.
- Put on the social, going-out outfit.

7.30 pm

- Moving from the one point, walk slowly to the kitchen.
- Place the prepared meal on a tray.
- Carry the tray into the designated space.
- Sit in the chair.
- Place the tray on your lap.
- Place palms approximately 10 cm above the food.
- Think of all the energy involved in getting the food onto your plate.
- Think of all the people involved in the chain that made it possible.
- Think of the forces of nature required for the food to exist.
- Think of how painful it is to starve.
- Be thankful for the food you are about to eat.
- Let the essence of that gratitude, stream out through your palms into the food.
- Eat dinner.
- Chew each mouthful 18 times.
- The only thought in your mind is, 'I am eating dinner'.
- When you've finished, stand up slowly.
- Moving from the one point, walk slowly to the kitchen.
- Place the tray down.

7.55 pm

- Walk to the designated space.
- Stand facing north, feet together, arms by your sides.
- Keep breathing.
- Watch yourself doing it from the centre of your brain.
- Slowly bend your knees a little.

235

- Tuck in your sacral bone.
- Lengthen your spine from waist-level down.
- Drop your chin and soften the back of your neck.
- Place your hands, palms facing up, at waist height in front of you, as if holding a large bowl, forefingers in line with the one point.
- Maintain enough space in each armpit to fit a small apple.
- Sensitize yourself to the energy flowing along your spine from the sacral bone at the base to the upper brainstem.
- Sensitize yourself to the energy flowing between your hands.
- Sensitize yourself to the energy field emanating from the one point below your navel and surrounding you up to a distance of 3 m from your physical periphery: above, below, behind, before and to the sides of you.
- Keep breathing.
- Watch yourself doing it all from the centre of your brain.

8.00 pm

- Say out loud 6 times, 'This energy protects me'.
- Slowly raise your palms to chest height.
- Make a fist in your right hand, palm-side facing your chest.
- Place your left palm on the outside of your right fist to shield it.
- Bow to the north.
- Bow to the east.
- Bow to the south.
- Bow to the west.
- Turn off the lights as required.
- Take your keys, money, a phone, which you should leave in the 'off' position to use only in case of emergencies, this book and anything else required for a low-key social occasion.

8.10 pm

- Leave the building.
- If having done the training accompanied, speak to your fellow participants if you feel a need.
- Act naturally.
- Keep breathing.
- Relax.
- Go somewhere unfamiliar in the vicinity or within a short drive, where you'll be required to talk to and interact, to some extent, with others in a social environment, where there'll be a bit of noise and colour for approximately 1 hour.
- There is no need to look at any clocks, wristwatches or other timepieces.
- Let your unconscious mind keep track of the time for you.
- The chosen venue could be a bar, pub or club – preferably somewhere you never or rarely frequent and wouldn't normally think of frequenting.
- As you walk in, tell yourself, you are nothing but energy, vibrating at sufficient frequency to hold your physical form in shape.
- Keep repeating this to yourself: 'I am nothing but energy, vibrating at sufficient frequency to hold this physical form in shape'.
- Let your gaze fall discreetly on each of the people present, one by one.
- Take your time.
- As your gaze falls on each person, tell yourself, they are nothing but energy, vibrating at sufficient frequency to hold their physical form in shape.
- Engage in whatever commerce is required in observing appropriate protocol.
- If this requires buying a drink, it's recommended to keep it alcohol free.
- If that could cause undue stress, keep it to one glass of something light.
- Introduce yourself to at least one person you don't know, preferably the one you'd be most scared to normally.
- As you approach them, remind yourself, they are nothing but energy, vibrating at sufficient frequency to hold their physical form in shape.
- Assure them warmly you're not an oddball or cult-member.

237

- Explain you're doing personal development training and are required to talk to someone you don't know, whom you'd normally be too afraid to approach.
- Show them the book.
- Point to this instruction.
- Have a laugh together.
- If the conversation goes no further, take your leave warmly and politely.
- Watch yourself doing it all from the centre of your brain.
- Relax.
- Keep breathing.
- Keep repeating to yourself: 'I am nothing but energy, vibrating at sufficient frequency to hold this physical form in shape'.
- If you enjoyed that so much you'd like to repeat it, do so with the second most scary-looking person there and so on.

9.45 pm

- Go home.

10.00 pm

- Check the time.
- Change from your social outfit into the brighter of the two indoor outfits.
- Say out loud, 'Life is getting brighter now'.
- Walk to the bathroom.
- Empty your bladder and bowels as required.

- Wash.

10.10 pm

- Moving from the one point below your navel, walk slowly to the kitchen.
- Drink water.
- As you do, your only thought is, 'I am drinking water'.
- Wash up the dinner dishes or rinse and place in the dishwasher.

10.20 pm

- Moving from the point below your navel, walk slowly to the designated space.
- Set the lighting.
- Spread the blanket on the floor.
- Lie down (without the book), knees bent, soles of the feet flat on the floor, arms by your sides.
- Even if you feel happy, start moaning out loud.
- Even if you have nothing in the entire universe to moan about, simply method-act your way into it. Use your whole body to express the emotion.
- If your moan wants to turn into a full-blown groan, let it.
- Moan for all the pain you've ever felt.
- Moan for all the times you deluded yourself you weren't enough.
- Moan for all the times you excluded yourself from the party.
- Moan for all the times you mistakenly thought you were all alone.
- Moan for all the times you were hard on yourself for no reason.
- Moan for all the things you regret.
- Moan for all the things you fear.
- Moan for all the existential angst you've ever felt.
- Moan for the sake of moaning.
- Moan for the suffering of all humankind.
- Moan for the suffering of all life.

10.35 pm

- Stop moaning.
- Relax your body.
- Lie still.
- If you want to laugh, laugh.
- If you want to cry, cry.
- Either way, keep breathing.
- Watch yourself doing it from deep inside the centre of your brain.
- Remind yourself, 'I am nothing but energy, vibrating at sufficient frequency to hold this physical form in shape'.
- Orientate yourself around the idea that as nothing but energy, vibrating at sufficient frequency to hold your physical form in shape, you are free and able to inform that energy with any qualities you see fit.
- Tell yourself, '… and that's precisely what I'm going to do tomorrow'.

10.55 pm

- Moving from the one point, roll to your left onto all fours.
- Let your head hang down.
- Soften the back of your neck.
- Keep breathing.
- Slowly stand up.
- Face approximately due north.
- Stand with feet at shoulder-width, arms hanging by your sides.
- Bend your knees slightly.
- Tuck your sacral bone under slightly.
- Lengthen your spine from waist-level down.
- Drop your chin and soften the back of your neck.

- Lengthen your spine from shoulder-level up.
- Keep breathing.
- Moving from the one point, rotate your forearms till your palms face forward. Bend at the elbows slightly.
- Raise your arms and open them outwards in a wide-embrace position.
- Relax your shoulders.
- Keep breathing.
- Visualize all the new that is coming to you – the mystery of the unknown – as a brightly coloured gaseous force with an appealing scent, swirling about in front of you.
- In the spirit of true hospitality, welcome it into your life.
- Using the inhalation as a mental trigger, draw it in through the centre of each palm, along each arm, through each shoulder, down through your chest and into your belly.
- Repeat 9 full inhalation–exhalation cycles, progressively welcoming the new more and more with each cycle.
- As your arms grow tired, relax your shoulders more.
- Out loud, say, 'It's all new from here'.
- Lower your arms slowly, until down by your sides.
- Rotate your forearms back till your palms face in.
- Relax your elbows.
- Straighten your legs.
- Place your feet together.
- Slowly swing both arms forward and raise to chest-level.
- Make a fist in your right hand.
- Place your left palm over your right fist to shield it.
- Bow to the north.
- Turn and bow to the east.
- Turn and bow to the south.
- Turn and bow to the west.
- Turn off lights as required.

11.15 pm

- Moving from the one point, walk to the kitchen.
- Drink water and prepare any bedtime drinks or snacks.
- Take any bedtime drinks or snacks to your sleeping place.
- Walk to the bathroom.
- Undress.
- Empty your bladder and bowels as required.
- Wash and take care of the essentials.
- Put on nightwear.

11.30 pm

- Walk to your sleeping place.
- Set the alarm to go off at 8.30 am.
- Get into bed.
- Lie back against the pillows, facing up.
- Keep breathing.
- Decelerate your breathing.
- Tell yourself, 'I now sleep deeply through the night and remain conscious as I dream and awake 6 full minutes before the alarm rings, feeling refreshed, rejuvenated, revitalized and ready for anything'.
- Read the following instructions 3 times carefully from, 'place the book down', up to, 'pick up the book and open it', and memorize.
- Mark your place in the book.
- Place the book down.
- Turn off the light.
- Close your eyes.
- Take stock of where you are and how you feel.

- Sink your consciousness back into the centre of your brain.
- As if you had a third eye in the centre of your forehead, gaze out through it at the darkened room.
- Just before falling fully asleep, turn onto your right side.

sunday (or third day of training)

reconstruction: the reharnessing process

8.24 am

- Wake up.
- Take stock of where you are and how you feel.
- Pick the book up and open it.
- Tell yourself, 'I choose to enjoy this day come what may' 6 times.
- Lightly place the tip of the forefinger of each hand at the outer corners of your eyes on each side.
- Stroke ever so softly and slowly along the edge of the bone immediately under each eye until your fingertips are touching the top of your nose on each side by the inner corner of each eye.
- Stroke softly and slowly along the edge of the bone immediately above each eye until your fingertips are once again at the outside corner of each eye.
- Repeat this cycle slowly, softly and patiently 18 times.
- The only thought in your mind is counting the cycles.

8.30 am

- Rolling to one side or the other, slowly get out of bed.
- Moving your body from the one point 6 cm below your navel, walk slowly to the bathroom.
- The only thought in your mind is, 'I'm walking slowly to the bathroom'.
- Empty your bladder and bowels as required.
- Wash, shower and take care of all the essentials.
- Dry off and put on the brighter of the two indoor lounging outfits.

9.30 am

- Moving from the one point 6 cm below your navel, walk slowly to the kitchen.
- The only thoughts in your mind are, 'I am walking slowly to the kitchen' and 'I have given this all the value it has for me', in respect of whatever your gaze falls upon.
- Make hot and cold beverages as required and drink.

9.45 am

- Set the alarm in the kitchen for 10.17 am.
- Do whatever you like till the alarm rings.
- Do not eat.
- Do not leave the house.
- Your only thought is, 'I am now doing whatever I like'.

10.17 am

- Walk into the designated space.
- Stand with feet together facing approximately due north.
- Place hands together in 'prayer' position.
- Bow to the north.
- Turn and bow to the east.
- Turn and bow to the south.
- Turn and bow to the west.
- Whatever your gaze falls upon, tell yourself, 'I am giving this all the positive value it has for me'.
- Set the lighting and temperature as required.
- Arrange blanket on the floor.
- Lie down on your back, knees bent, soles of your feet flat on the floor.
- Allow your lower back to broaden and sink into the floor.
- Keep breathing.
- Place your arms by your sides.
- Moving from the one point 6 cm below your navel, slowly raise your torso off the floor until you feel the muscles in your belly contract.
- Keep breathing.
- Relax all muscle groups not being actively used in the raising motion, especially the back of your neck.
- Hold the posture.
- Breathe slowly.
- Count 18 cycles of inhalation and exhalation.
- Lower your torso slowly till your entire back is lying flat again.
- Let your lower back sink into the floor.
- Lengthen your spine.
- Relax everything.
- Keep breathing.
- Count 3 cycles of inhalation and exhalation.

- Repeat the entire process of raising and lowering the torso 9 times.

- Place your palms on your belly.
- Mentally repeat the word 'strength' 9 times.
- Turn onto your front.
- Stretch your legs out straight behind you, feet together.
- Place your palms on the floor, just to the outside of your shoulders.
- Lengthen your spine, especially the back of your neck.
- Keep breathing.
- Pull your buttocks and the muscles of your lower back inwards towards the spine.
- Moving from the one point below your navel, slowly raise your torso approximately 10 cm from the floor.
- Maintain the inward pull of the buttocks and lower back muscles.
- Relax all other muscle groups, especially at the back of the neck.
- Breathe more slowly.
- Count 9 cycles of inhalation and exhalation.
- Lower your torso slowly to the floor.
- Repeat the sequence 3 times through.
- Focusing awareness on your buttocks and lower back, mentally repeat the word 'strength' 9 times.
- Roll to your right and lie on your back.
- Bend your legs at the knees.
- Place your soles flat on the floor, legs together.
- Stretch your arms out to the sides perpendicular to your torso to form a 'T'.
- Turn your head to face your right hand.
- Turning from the one point below your navel, let your legs slowly fall over to the left until your left knee is on the floor.
- Keep breathing.
- Feel the stretch across your torso.
- Breathe more slowly.
- Count 9 cycles of inhalation and exhalation.
- Moving from the one point below your navel, slowly draw your legs straight and turn your head till gazing up at the ceiling.

247

- Turn your head to face your left hand.
- Turning from the one point below your navel, let your legs slowly fall over to the right until your right knee is on the floor.
- Keep breathing.
- Feel the stretch across your torso.
- Breathe more slowly.
- Count 9 cycles of inhalation and exhalation.
- Moving from the one point below your navel, slowly draw your legs straight and turn your head till gazing up at the ceiling.
- Place both palms on your chest.
- Mentally repeat the word 'strength' 9 times.
- Roll to your left.
- Come onto all fours.
- Let your head hang down.
- Relax the back of your neck.
- Keep breathing.
- Moving from the one point, slowly stand up.
- Fold and stow the blanket.

11.17 am

- Moving from the one point, walk slowly to the bathroom.
- Empty your bladder and bowels as required.
- Relax.
- Keep breathing.
- Wash.

11.30 am

- Moving from the one point, walk slowly to the kitchen.
- The only thought in your mind is, 'I am walking slowly to the kitchen'.
- Prepare breakfast.
- The only thought in your mind is, 'I am preparing breakfast'.
- Place palms approximately 10 cm above the food.
- Think of all the energy involved in getting the food onto your plate.
- Think of all the people involved in the chain that made it possible.
- Think of the forces of nature required for the food to exist.
- Think of how painful it is to starve.
- Be thankful for the food you are about to eat.
- Let the essence of that gratitude, stream out through your palms into the food.
- Eat breakfast.
- Chew each mouthful 18 times.
- The only thought in your mind is, 'I am eating breakfast'.

12.00 pm

- Moving from the one point, walk slowly to the designated space.
- Take the pad and pen.
- Sit in the chair.
- Relax.
- Keep breathing.
- Lengthen your spine.
- Broaden your hips and shoulders.
- Allowing one entire page for each, make a list of the following personal attributes, (placing one attribute as a header at the top of each page):

249

'*Always-on willingness and readiness to perceive, acknowledge and accept the paradox inherent in every aspect of existence and to appreciate its significance, especially when things appear to be moving against you.*'

'*Always-on willingness and readiness to exercise the resilience to optimize conditions, as they present themselves – to always see and make the most of your external reality, especially in the face of disappointment and deflation.*'

'*Always-on willingness and readiness to relax your body and mind and to breathe freely and, where possible, slowly, especially in the midst of stressful situations.*'

'*Always-on willingness and readiness to access and activate the courage to continue contributing to the world around you and letting it contribute to you, especially when it or you feels irrelevant.*'

'*Always-on willingness and readiness to enter a state of full surrender to the pull of the mystery, especially when apparently stepping into the abyss.*'

'*Always-on willingness and readiness to clear and focus your mind by repositioning your internal stance in relation to reality, especially during stressful phases of information and responsibility overload.*'

'*Always-on willingness and readiness to touch the world with love, by exercising humaneness, compassion, humour, kindness, fairness, mercy and forgiveness in your dealings, both with others and with your own self, especially when confronted by prejudice, meanness and pettiness, either in others or yourself.*'

'Always-on willingness and readiness to be humble enough to listen and quiet enough to hear the still small voice of the spirit within you and wise enough to do what it tells you, especially when it apparently runs counter to the strict demands of your rational mind.'

'Always-on willingness and readiness to access and exercise tenacious strength and limitless stamina in order to follow through and complete, especially when faced with an apparently insurmountable obstacle.'

'Always-on willingness and readiness to retreat to the fallback position of knowing you are nothing but pure energy, vibrating at the appropriate set of frequencies to hold you in shape – that in the ultimate sense, you, as you've come to know yourself, do not exist at all, especially when your very existence is threatened.'

'Always-on willingness and readiness to be sincere in all your dealings with others and yourself, especially when confronted by dishonesty and insincerity in others or yourself.'

'Always-on willingness and readiness to dedicate your life to serving the greater flow of energy expressed in humankind at large, especially when tempted by the glitter of personal gain or glory.'

'Always-on willingness and readiness to cease attempting to draw conclusions, especially when apparently being forced to make a decision or take a position.'

'Always-on willingness and readiness to let go of your version of how reality is or should be, especially when it appears your survival depends on you defining your reality.'

- Flip back through the pages and carefully read each of the above 3 times, focusing on the meaning as it occurs to you (as opposed to trancing out).

12.30 pm

- Moving from the one point, slowly place the pad by your side.
- Stand up.
- Stand facing north, feet together, arms by your sides, palms facing in.
- Slowly rotate your forearms to position your palms facing outwards.
- Bend your elbows slightly.
- Slowly raise your arms out to the sides to shoulder-level, as if holding up a 2-m long log across your chest.
- Keep breathing.
- Relax.
- With your arms in log-carrying position, turn to your right.
- Moving from the one point, walk slowly in a clockwise circle just within the periphery of the designated space.
- As your weight falls through your left foot, place awareness in your right hand.
- As your weight falls through your right foot, place awareness in your left hand.
- Sensitize yourself to the energy flowing between your two palms.
- As your arms grow tired, relax your shoulders more.
- Keep breathing.
- Your only thought is, 'I am stepping into the new now'.
- Complete 36 circuits.
- Stop and stand, feet together, facing north.
- Slowly, moving from the one point, lower your arms to your sides and rotate your forearms until your palms face in.
- Say out loud, 'I am ready and willing to take on the new now'.

1.00 pm

- Sit in the chair.
- Pick up the pad and pen.
- Turn to the page headed, 'Always-on willingness and readiness to perceive, acknowledge and accept the paradox inherent in every aspect of existence and to appreciate its significance, especially when things appear to be moving against you'.
- Beneath it, write, 'I am now willing and ready to perceive, acknowledge and accept the paradox inherent in every aspect of my existence and to a appreciate its significance, especially when things appear to be moving against me'.
- Then write it again and again until you've filled the entire page with it.
- Do this without thinking. Just write.
- Repeat this process with each of the headings, writing the following affirmations respectively:

> *'I am now willing and ready to exercise the resilience to optimize conditions, as they present themselves – to always see and make the most of my external reality, especially in the face of disappointment and deflation.'*

> *'I am now willing and ready to relax my body and mind and to breathe freely and, where possible, slowly, especially in the midst of stressful situations.'*

> *'I am now willing and ready to access and activate the courage to continue contributing to the world around me and letting it contribute to me, especially when it or I feel irrelevant.'*

> *'I am now willing and ready to enter a state of full surrender to the pull of the mystery, especially when apparently stepping into the abyss.'*

253

'I am now willing and ready to clear and focus my mind by repositioning my internal stance in relation to reality, especially during stressful phases of information and responsibility overload.'

'I am now willing and ready to touch the world with love, by exercising humaneness, compassion, humour, kindness, fairness, mercy and forgiveness in my dealings, both with others and with my own self, especially when confronted by prejudice, meanness and pettiness, either in others or myself.'

'I am now willing and ready to be humble enough to listen and quiet enough to hear the still small voice of the spirit within me and wise enough to do what it tells me, especially when it apparently runs counter to the strict demands of my rational mind.'

'I am now willing and ready to access and exercise tenacious strength and limitless stamina in order to follow through and complete, especially when faced with an apparently insurmountable obstacle.'

'I am now willing and ready to retreat to the fallback position of knowing I am nothing but pure energy, vibrating at the appropriate set of frequencies to hold me in shape – that in the ultimate sense, I, as I've come to know myself, do not exist at all – this, especially when my very existence is threatened.'

'I am now willing and ready to be sincere in all my dealings with others and myself, especially when confronted by dishonesty and insincerity in others or myself.'

'I am now willing and ready to dedicate my life to serving the greater flow of energy expressed in humankind at large, especially when tempted by the glitter of personal gain or glory.'

'I am now willing and ready to cease attempting to draw conclusions, especially when apparently being forced to make a decision or take a position.'

'I am now willing and ready to let go of my version of how reality is or should be, especially when it appears my survival depends on me defining my reality.'

1.30 pm

- Place the pad down by your side.
- Moving from your centre, stand and walk slowly to the bathroom.
- Empty your bladder and bowels as required.
- Wash.
- Look at your face in the mirror.
- Out loud, say, 'I love you'.
- Walk slowly to the designated space.
- Stand facing north, feet spread as wide apart as you can get them, knees lightly bent.
- Drop slowly forward from the hips.
- Place your palms on the floor in front on you, shoulder-width apart, arms straight.
- Exhale fully.
- Inhale slowly, bend your arms and slowly bring your chest towards the floor, allowing your heels to come off the floor.
- Exhale and slowly straighten your arms, pushing your hips backwards until back in the original position.
- Repeat twice more.
- Your only thought is, 'I'm doing this to grow stronger'.

- Moving from the centre, draw yourself slowly upright.
- Inhale.
- Exhale and jump your feet together.
- Stand with feet together, arms hanging at your sides.
- Bend your knees lightly.
- Tuck your sacrum under to lengthen your spine from waist-level down.
- Drop your chin slightly to lengthen your spine from shoulder-level up.
- Make fists.
- Nestle your left fist into your left hip joint.
- From the one point, turn a bit to the left and place your right fist on top of your left fist, to form a small cross.
- Using the intersection formed by your two wrists as a lining-up point, gaze down at the floor.
- Keep breathing.
- Allow stillness to flood you.
- Your only thought is, 'I am still – I am strong'.
- Count to 180.
- Repeat on the other side, placing your left wrist on top of your right.
- Sit down.
- Pick up the pad.
- Read each page aloud, reciting every repetition of each affirmation as many times as it appears on the page.
- Emphasize different syllables in different words at random with each repetition.
- Allow the meaning of each affirmation to impact on your psyche.
- Detach the lists.
- Stow the lists.
- Place the pad by your side.
- Moving from the one point, slowly stand.

2.00 pm

- Set alarm to go off at 2.33 pm.
- Spread the blanket.
- Place the book-as-pillow accordingly.
- Lie down, knees bent, soles flat on the floor, arms by your sides.
- Keep breathing.
- Relax your shoulders.
- Make fists.
- Place fists just over each side of the centre of your breastbone.
- Take stock of where you are and how you feel.
- Inhale deeply.
- Exhale, chanting the sound, 'HAAAAAAAH!' resonantly until all the air is emptied from your lungs.
- Repeat this 8 more times.
- Simultaneously pummel your chest gently but firmly.
- Keep your shoulders relaxed.
- At the end of the last of the 9 exhalations, stop pummelling suddenly.
- Sensitize yourself to the fizzing sensation in your chest.
- Place awareness in your palms.
- Keep breathing.
- On each inhalation, feel your life-force gathering around the one point below your navel.
- On each exhalation, feel your life-force travel in two separate streams up to your shoulders, down your arms and into your palms.
- Your only thought is, 'Compassion keeps me safe'.

2.33 pm

- Moving from the one point, slowly roll to your right and up onto all fours.
- Let your head hang down.
- Tuck your sacrum slightly under.
- Feel your spine elongate.
- Keep breathing.
- Your only thought is, 'I am breathing'.
- Take stock of where you are and how you feel.
- Slowly stand, fold and stow the blanket and book, face north, feet at shoulder-width, arms hanging naturally by your sides.
- Keep breathing.
- Bend your knees lightly.
- Tuck your sacrum slightly under.
- Tuck your chin slightly in.
- Elongate your spine from waist-level down and from shoulder-level up.
- Turn your right foot out to a 45° angle.
- Moving from the one point, lean your full body weight on your right foot.
- Step your left foot directly forward facing due north.
- Transfer your body weight fully onto your left foot.
- Moving from the one point, draw your body weight back onto your right foot and step your left foot back behind your right foot, placing it down, toes first facing out at a 45° angle (north-west).
- Transfer all your body weight onto your right foot.
- Moving from the one point, draw your body weight back onto your left foot again and step into the forward stance – then back, then forward and so on, until you feel the momentum of your one point moving back and forth in space is causing you to advance and retreat without effort.
- As you advance and retreat, let your arms swing naturally as a counterweight.
- Step forwards and backwards like this 180 times.
- Change sides with a hop (so now your right foot will be stepping to and fro) and repeat likewise 180 times.

- Your only thought is, 'I am advancing and retreating with balance, poise and grace'.
- Stand with feet parallel at shoulder-width, knees bent, sacrum tucked under, chin tucked in.
- Keep breathing.
- Allow your energy to sink and settle around the one point.
- Your only thought is, 'Here I stand strong'.

3.12 pm

- Set the alarm for 4 pm.
- Spread the blanket and place the book-as-pillow.
- Lie down, knees up, soles flat, arms by your sides.
- Read carefully 3 times and memorize the following instructions from 'place the book down' up to 'pick the book up'.
- Place the book down.
- Close your eyes.
- Sink into the awareness of being just your bones.
- With that, incorporate awareness of being flesh.
- With that, incorporate awareness of being fluids.
- With that, incorporate awareness of being nerves.
- With that, incorporate awareness of being energy.
- With that, incorporate awareness of being consciousness.
- With that, incorporate awareness of being spirit.
- With that, incorporate awareness of being love.
- With that, incorporate awareness of being invincible.
- With that, incorporate awareness of simultaneously being human.
- Hold all this awareness simultaneously.
- Keep breathing.

4.00 pm

- Pick the book up.
- Take stock of where you are and how you feel.
- Stand slowly, facing north, feet together, arms hanging naturally by your sides.
- Draw your awareness back into the centre of your brain and witness the following from there.
- Keep breathing.
- With its epicentre in the one point below your navel, envision an egg-shaped, light-filled energy field surrounding and extending out from the physical parameters of your body by 2 m, above, below, behind, before and to the sides of you.
- See this field comprised of two interfusing sub-fields, moving through each other, each spinning around you in opposite directions, clockwise and counterclockwise at the speed of light – 186,000 miles per second.
- Your only thought is, 'This energy is protecting me'.

4.12 pm

- Moving slowly from the one point, bow to the north, east, south and west respectively, turn off lighting as required and walk to the bathroom.
- Empty your bladder and bowels as required.
- Wash.
- Change into outdoor clothes and footwear.
- Walk slowly to the kitchen.
- Drink water.
- Take stock of where you are and how you feel.
- Check the time.

- Tell your unconscious mind to keep track of the time and return you home by 5.30 pm.
- Gather your keys, money, this book and mobile phone (to be kept in the 'off' position except for use in an emergency) and stow them on your person.
- Leave the building.
- Turn right.
- Walk approximately 3 km round the block in a clockwise direction.
- If no block is available to walk, go approximately 1.5 km and turn back.
- Whatever your gaze falls upon, tell yourself, 'I have imbued this with the beauty and light I see in it'.
- Whomever you pass, see or meet, think, 'I have imbued this person with the beauty and light I see in them'.
- Unthreateningly, humbly instigate polite eye contact with whomever you pass or meet.
- Open your mind to the possibility of striking up conversation with anyone you pass or encounter, including total strangers and make yourself energetically available to it should the opportunity arise.
- If the opportunity does arise to converse with a stranger or someone you know, place your right palm on your solar plexus (upper abdomen) while you talk, keep breathing and witness the proceedings from the centre of your brain.
- Should this situation arise, choose to see only the potentially positive qualities in the person or people you engage with.
- Whichever qualities you see in them, tell yourself, 'I have imbued this person with this quality I see in them'.

5.30 pm

- Walk back in the building.
- Change back into the brighter indoor outfit.

- Walk to the bathroom.
- Empty your bladder and bowels as required.
- Wash.
- Walk to the designated space.
- Set the lighting as required.
- Stand facing north, feet together.
- Bow to the north, east, south and west.
- Walk to the kitchen.
- Prepare a snack – as energy rich as possible – and some tea.
- Place snack and tea on a tray.
- Moving from the one point, carry the tray into the designated space.
- Sit carefully in the chair.
- Place the tray on your lap.
- Hold your hands approximately 10 cm above the food, palms down.
- Be aware of all the people and energy involved along the chain, responsible for this food being on your plate.
- Feel gratitude.
- Let this gratitude be transmitted through your palms into the food.
- Eat the snack.
- Chew each mouthful 18 times.
- Your only thought is, 'I am chewing this food – I have imbued it with all the enjoyment it has for me'.
- Drink the tea.
- Stand carefully.
- Take the tray back into the kitchen.
- Walk to the designated space.
- Sit on your heels.
- If this is uncomfortable, sit in the chair and push your buttocks firmly into the seat.
- Sensitize yourself to the sensation of your stomach processing the information contained in the food.
- Keep breathing.
- Place your right palm on your solar plexus (upper abdomen).

- Feel the warmth of your palm penetrate your stomach.
- Envision the midday sun shining there, lighting up the whole of the inside of your body.
- Envision this light extending to fill your entire egg-shaped energy field, above, below, before, behind and to the sides of you.
- Your only thought is, 'I am this light'.

6.00 pm

- Take stock of where you are and how you feel.
- Moving from the one point, walk slowly to the bathroom.
- Empty your bladder and bowels as required.
- Wash and take care of the essentials.
- Change into your low-key social event outfit.
- Walk to the designated space.
- Take the mirror.
- Sit in the chair.
- Keep breathing.
- Tuck in your chin slightly to elongate your spine from shoulder-level up.
- Tuck in your sacrum slightly to elongate your spine from waist-level down.
- Broaden across your shoulder and hip girdles.
- Soften your muscles, especially the back of your neck and your buttocks.
- Relax your shoulders, elbows and wrists and hold the mirror so you can gaze into your own eyes.
- Read carefully 3 times and memorize the following instructions from 'draw your consciousness back into the centre of your brain' up to 'sharpen your gaze and bring your reflection back into focus'.
- Draw your consciousness back into the centre of your brain and gaze at the reflection of your eyes from there.

263

- Allow your features to dissolve until you disappear.
- Your only thought is, 'I am pure energy'.
- Expand your scope of vision to take in your entire energy field.
- Your only thought is, 'Pure energy is invincible'.
- Place awareness in the one point below your navel.
- Keep breathing.
- Concentrate your consciousness in the centre of your brain.
- Your only thought is, 'I am pure spirit'.
- Expand your consciousness to fill your entire egg-shaped energy field.
- Your only thought is, 'Pure spirit is invincible'.
- Keep breathing.
- Sharpen your gaze and bring your reflection back into focus.
- Place the mirror down.

6.23 pm

- Moving from the one point, stand up.
- Stand facing north with feet shoulder-width apart, arms hanging by your sides.
- Bend your knees slightly.
- Tuck in your chin slightly to elongate your spine from shoulder-level up.
- Tuck in your sacrum slightly to elongate your spine from waist-level down.
- Broaden across your shoulder and hip girdles.
- Soften your muscles.
- Keep breathing.
- Breathe more slowly.
- For the duration of 9 slow inhalation–exhalation cycles, gently shake your fingertips as if shaking off water.
- Transfer all your body-weight onto your left foot.

- Raise your right foot a few centimetres off the ground.
- For the duration of 3 slow inhalation–exhalation cycles, shake the toes of your right foot as if shaking off water.
- Place your right foot down.
- Shift your entire body-weight onto your right foot.
- Raise your left foot a few centimetres off the ground.
- For the duration of 3 slow inhalation–exhalation cycles, shake the toes of your left foot as if shaking off water.
- Place your left foot down.
- Transfer your body-weight until it's falling 50 per cent through each foot.
- Bend your elbows slightly.
- Raise both arms straight out in front, palms out, as if pushing against a wall.
- Keep breathing.
- Maintain the posture for the duration of 9 slow inhalation–exhalation cycles.
- With each inhalation, envision energy gathering around the one point, forming a compressed ball of light.
- With each exhalation, envision releasing enough energy from the ball of light around the one point, to travel up in two streams, one to each shoulder, then down along the outside of each arm, into the centre of each palm and out into infinity beyond in two straight lines of infinite length.
- Lower your arms slowly.
- Straighten your legs.

7.03 pm

- Sit on your heels. (If this is difficult, sit in the chair and push your buttocks back into the seat).
- Take stock of where you are and how you feel.
- Make fists.

- Relax your shoulders, elbows and wrists.
- Keep breathing.
- Place your fists in front of your chest.
- Pummel your chest gently.
- Simultaneously, chant the sound, 'HAAAAAAAH!' as continuously and with the most possible resonance.
- Continue for the duration of 9 slow inhalation–exhalation cycles.
- Towards the end of the last cycle, stop pummelling suddenly.
- Sensitize yourself to the fizzing sensation in your chest.
- Allow it to spread throughout your body.
- Your only thought is, 'I am pure love'.
- Keep breathing.
- Allow it to spread beyond your physical parameters and fill your entire egg-shaped energy field.
- Your only thought is, 'Pure love is invincible'.

7.23 pm

- Moving from the one point, stand facing north, feet together, arms by your sides.
- Rotate your forearms back till your palms face in.
- Relax your elbows.
- Slowly swing both arms forward and raise to chest-level.
- Make a fist in your right hand.
- Place your left palm over your right fist to shield it.
- Bow to the north.
- Turn and bow to the east.
- Turn and bow to the south.
- Turn and bow to the west.

- Turn off lights as required.
- Gather your keys, money, this book, and a mobile phone in case of emergency.
- Go somewhere unfamiliar in the vicinity or within a short drive, where you'll be required to talk to and interact, to some extent, with others in a social environment, where there'll be a bit of noise and colour for approximately 1 hour.
- There is no need to look at any clocks, wristwatches or other timepieces.
- Let your unconscious mind keep track of the time for you.
- The chosen venue could be a bar, pub or club – preferably not the same venue as yesterday evening. Somewhere you never or rarely frequent and wouldn't normally think of frequenting.
- As you walk in, tell yourself that you are nothing but pure love in action.
- Keep repeating this to yourself: 'I am nothing but pure love in action'.
- Let your gaze fall discreetly on each of the people present, one by one.
- Take your time.
- As your gaze falls on each person, tell yourself that they are nothing but pure love in action.
- Engage in whatever commerce is required in observing appropriate conventional protocol.
- If this requires buying a drink, it's recommended to keep it alcohol free.
- If that could cause undue stress, keep it to one glass of something light.
- Introduce yourself to at least one person you don't know – preferably the one you'd be most scared to normally and not the one you spoke to yesterday evening.
- As you approach them, remind yourself, they are nothing but pure love in action.
- Assure them warmly you're not an oddball or cult-member.
- Explain you're doing personal development training and are required to talk to someone you don't know, whom you'd normally be too afraid to approach.
- Show them the book.
- Point to this instruction.
- Have a laugh together.
- If the conversation goes no further of its own accord, take your leave warmly and politely and move on to engaging the second most scary person for you.

- Watch yourself doing it all from the centre of your brain.
- Relax.
- Keep breathing.
- Keep repeating to yourself, 'I am nothing but pure love in action'.

9.00 pm

- Go home.

9.23 pm

- Change into your bright indoor outfit.
- Walk to the bathroom.
- Empty your bladder and bowels as required.
- Walk to the designated space.
- Set lighting and heating as required.
- Moving from the one point, stand, facing north, feet together, arms by your sides.
- Rotate your forearms back till your palms face in.
- Relax your elbows.
- Slowly swing both arms forward and raise to chest-level.
- Make a fist in your right hand.
- Place your left palm over your right fist to shield it.
- Bow to the north.
- Turn and bow to the east.
- Turn and bow to the south.
- Turn and bow to the west.
- Walk to the kitchen.

- Prepare a very light, easily digestible meal.

- Place meal on a tray.
- Moving from the one point, carry the tray into the designated space.
- Sit carefully in the chair.
- Place the tray on your lap.
- Hold your hands approximately 10 cm above the food, palms down.
- Be aware of all the people and energy involved along the chain, responsible for this food being on your plate.
- Feel gratitude.
- Let this gratitude be transmitted through your palms into the food.
- Eat the food.
- Chew each mouthful 18 times.
- Your only thought is, 'I am chewing this food – I have imbued it with all the enjoyment it has for me'.
- Stand carefully.
- Take the tray back into the kitchen.
- Walk to the designated space.

10.23 pm

- Sit in the chair.
- Sensitize yourself to the digestive process occurring in your gastro-intestinal tract.
- Take stock of where you are and how you feel.
- Reread aloud the contract you wrote out, signed and stowed.

'I, [your name here], do hereby solemnly swear to take myself through this training from start to end in one go, following the instructions precisely to the letter. I accept there will be difficult moments and passages and yet am willing to persevere regardless'.

10.30 pm

- Keep breathing.
- Relax your muscles.
- Tuck your sacrum under to lengthen your spine from waist-level down.
- Drop your chin slightly to lengthen your spine from shoulder-level up.
- Touch all four fingertips of your right hand to the tip of your right thumb to form a bird's beak shape.
- Relax your shoulders, elbows and wrists.
- Slowly raise your right hand until the apex formed by fingertips and the tip of your thumb is in line with your gaze.
- Gaze at the apex.
- Sensitize yourself to the stream of subtle energy flowing through your eyes between the apex and the centre of your brain.
- Keep breathing.

10.40 pm

- Lower your right hand.
- Touch all four fingertips of your left hand to the tip of your left thumb to form the bird's beak.
- Relax your shoulders, elbows and wrists.
- Slowly raise your left hand until the apex formed by fingertips and the tip of your thumb is in line with your gaze.
- Gaze at the apex.
- Sensitize yourself to the stream of subtle energy flowing through your eyes between the apex and the centre of your brain.
- Keep breathing.

10.50 pm

- Lower your left hand.
- Visualize the planet.
- Visualize all the people.
- Keep breathing.
- Feel your consciousness expand.
- Feel your consciousness expand until it's larger than your body.
- Feel your consciousness expand until it feels as if you're looking at the world from 1 m above the crown of your head.
- See the same happen to the consciousness of everyone on the planet.
- See your consciousness meet the consciousness of everyone on the planet.
- See your consciousness and the consciousness of everyone combined form a sea of consciousness.
- See the entire planet enveloped in a sea of consciousness.
- Visualize an opening in the centre of your chest.
- Feel as if you're breathing in and out through this opening.
- Feel a stream of love radiate from your chest and penetrate the sea of consciousness.
- Keep breathing until the entire sea of consciousness enveloping the planet is completely suffused with love.
- Visualize openings in the centre of the sole of each foot.
- Feel as if you're breathing in and out through these openings.
- Feel streams of love radiate through the soles of your feet into the centre of the Earth until the entire planet is filled with love.
- Keep breathing.
- Relax your shoulders, elbows and wrists.
- Raise your arms straight out in front of you, palms facing out, to shoulder height as if pushing against a wall.
- Visualize openings in the centre of the palm of each hand.
- Feel as if you're breathing in and out through these openings.

- Feel streams of love radiate through your palms until you feel fully connected to all that is.
- Lower your arms.
- Relax and detach.
- Keep breathing.
- Take stock of where you are and how you feel.

11.15 pm

- Moving from the one point, stand, facing north, feet together, arms by your sides.
- Rotate your forearms back till your palms face in.
- Relax your elbows.
- Slowly swing both arms forward and raise to chest-level.
- Make a fist in your right hand.
- Place your left palm over your right fist to shield it.
- Bow to the north.
- Turn and bow to the east.
- Turn and bow to the south.
- Turn and bow to the west.
- Turn out the lights.
- Moving from the one point, walk to the kitchen.
- Drink water and prepare any bedtime drinks or snacks.
- Take any bedtime drinks or snacks to your sleeping place.
- Walk to the bathroom.
- Undress.
- Empty your bladder and bowels as required.
- Wash and take care of the essentials.

- Put on nightwear.

11.30 pm

- Walk to your sleeping place.
- Set the alarm to go off at your usual Monday morning wake-up time.
- Get into bed.
- Lie back against the pillows, facing up.
- Keep breathing.
- Decelerate your breathing.
- Tell yourself, 'I now sleep deeply through the night, remain consciously in command as I dream, fly if I want and awake 6 full minutes before the alarm rings, feeling refreshed, rejuvenated, revitalized and ready for something entirely new'.
- Read the following instructions 3 times carefully from 'place the book down' up to 'pick up the book and open it', and memorize.
- Mark your place in the book.
- Place the book down.
- Turn off the light.
- Close your eyes.
- Take stock of where you are and how you feel.
- Sink your consciousness back into the centre of your brain.
- As if you had a third eye in the centre of your forehead, gaze out through it at the darkened room.
- Just before falling fully asleep, turn onto your right side.

4 monday (or last day of training)

reconstructed: the reintegration process

- Wake up 6 minutes before the alarm.
- Take stock of where you are and how you feel.
- Pick the book up and open it.
- Tell yourself, 'I choose to enjoy this day come what may' 6 times.
- Lightly place the tip of the forefinger of each hand at the outer corners of your eyes on each side.
- Stroke ever so softly and slowly along the edge of the bone immediately under each eye until your fingertips are touching the top of your nose on each side by the inner corner of each eye.
- Stroke softly and slowly along the edge of the bone immediately above each eye until your fingertips are once again at the outside corner of each eye.
- Repeat this cycle slowly, softly and patiently 18 times.
- The only thought in your mind is counting the cycles.
- Moving your body from the one point 6 cm below your navel, walk slowly to the bathroom.
- The only thought in your mind is, 'I'm walking slowly to the bathroom'.
- Empty your bladder and bowels as required.
- From now till 10 am, do what you would normally on a Monday morning.
- Take this book with you wherever you go.
- Observe yourself from the centre of the brain.
- Keep breathing.
- Your only thought is, 'I am doing what I normally do'.

10.00 am

- Wherever you are, whomever you're with, whatever you're doing, take stock of where you are and what you feel like.
- Keep breathing.
- Relax your muscles.
- Tuck your sacrum under to lengthen your spine from waist-level down.
- Drop your chin slightly to lengthen your spine from shoulder-level up.
- Observe yourself from the centre of your brain.
- Soften your chest.
- Place awareness in the one point.
- Wherever you are, whomever you're with, whatever else you're doing, repeat this thought continuously so it becomes a repeated motif on the wallpaper of your mind: 'I am nothing but pure energy. Pure energy is invincible'.
- Whomever your gaze encounters, tell yourself, 'Whether they know it or not, this person is nothing but pure energy. Pure energy is invincible'.
- Whomever you chance upon, make eye contact and hold and touch lightly yet firmly on the upper arm for the length of one inhalation and exhalation, while saying hello.
- Otherwise carry on as normal.

10.37 am

- Wherever you are, whomever you're with, whatever you're doing, take stock of where you are and what you feel like.
- Keep breathing.
- Relax your muscles.
- Tuck your sacrum under to lengthen your spine from waist-level down.
- Drop your chin slightly to lengthen your spine from shoulder-level up.

275

- Observe yourself from the centre of your brain.
- Soften your chest.
- Place awareness in the one point.
- Wherever you are, whomever you're with, whatever else you're doing, repeat this thought continuously so it becomes a repeated motif on the wallpaper of your mind: 'I am nothing but pure consciousness. Pure consciousness is invincible'.
- Whomever your gaze encounters, tell yourself, 'Whether they know it or not, this person is nothing but pure consciousness. Pure consciousness is invincible.'
- Choose one person – anyone will do – and verbally acknowledge them for one fine quality you see in them. If necessary, because of stilted delivery on your part, or through the unusual nature of what you're saying within the context, show them this instruction in the book.
- Allow whatever conversation this inspires to evolve naturally.
- Keep breathing.
- Observe yourself from the centre of your brain.
- Otherwise carry on as you normally would.

11.07 am

- Wherever you are, whomever you're with, whatever you're doing, take stock of where you are and what you feel like.
- Keep breathing.
- Relax your muscles.
- Tuck your sacrum under to lengthen your spine from waist-level down.
- Drop your chin slightly to lengthen your spine from shoulder-level up.
- Observe yourself from the centre of your brain.
- Soften your chest.

- Place awareness in the one point.
- Wherever you are, whomever you're with, whatever else you're doing, repeat this thought continuously so it becomes a repeated motif on the wallpaper of your mind: 'I am nothing but pure love in action. Pure love in action is invincible'.
- Whomever your gaze encounters, tell yourself, 'Whether they know it or not, this person is nothing but pure love in action. Pure love in action is invincible'.
- Choose one person – anyone will do – and do something notably generous and kind for them.
- Do not expect or wait for thanks.
- Instead, inside, say, 'Thanks for this chance to serve'.
- Otherwise carry on as you normally would.

11.37 am

- Wherever you are, whomever you're with, whatever you're doing, take stock of where you are and what you feel like.
- Keep breathing.
- Relax your muscles.
- Tuck your sacrum under to lengthen your spine from waist-level down.
- Drop your chin slightly to lengthen your spine from shoulder-level up.
- Observe yourself from the centre of your brain.
- Soften your chest.
- Place awareness in the one point.
- Wherever you are, whomever you're with, whatever else you're doing, repeat this thought continuously so it becomes a repeated motif on the wallpaper of your mind: 'I am invincible'.
- Whomever your gaze encounters, tell yourself, 'Whether they know it or not, this person is invincible'.

12.00 pm

- Congratulations.
- You have completed the training.
- You may now consider yourself invincible.